EMPOWER YOUR INNER PSYCHIC

EMPOWER YOUR INNER PSYCHIC

HOW TO HARNESS YOUR INTUITION AND MANIFEST YOUR DREAM LIFE

THERESA CHEUNG

Thorsons

Harper Thorsons
An imprint of HarperCollins*Publishers*
1 London Bridge Street
London SE1 9GF

www.harpercollins.co.uk

HarperCollins*Publishers*
Macken House, 39/40 Mayor Street Upper
Dublin 1, D01 C9W8, Ireland

First published by Harper Thorsons 2023

1 3 5 7 9 10 8 6 4 2

© Theresa Cheung 2023

Theresa Cheung asserts the moral right to
be identified as the author of this work

A catalogue record of this book is
available from the British Library

ISBN 978-0-00-853649-7

Printed and bound in the UK using 100%
renewable electricity at CPI Group (UK) Ltd

To my wonderful readers past, present and future.
You are the stuff that dreams are made on.

Contents

'What you think you create.
What you feel you attract.
What you dream you become.'

It's your Psychic World

Einstein once said that the most beautiful thing we could experience in the world was the mysterious. Profound words indeed. But mystery isn't something you simply experience. Mystery defines *you.*

Your very existence on this Earth is an unsolved puzzle. Despite their best efforts, scientists still don't know for sure why humankind exists. The universe remains an enigma. But perhaps the greatest mystery of all is human consciousness, including your individual awareness of your own feelings, thoughts, memories, dreams and sensations. And discovering the unlimited potential of your own inner space is the greatest of all living adventures.

OUT THERE, IN HERE

American astronaut Edgar Mitchell was the sixth person to land on the moon. Returning from his final mission, with the Earth in sight, he had a profound sense of universal connectedness. In his own words:

> I realized that the story of ourselves as told by science, our
> cosmology, our religion, was likely flawed. I recognized that
> the Newtonian idea of separate, independent, discrete things
> in the universe wasn't a fully accurate description. What was

needed was a new story of who we are and what we are capable of becoming.

This transcendent experience utterly transformed Mitchell and he devoted the rest of his life to applying the scientific rigour used in his explorations of outer space to the mysteries of inner space – the space he felt an indisputable sense of oneness and interconnection with. He established the Institute of Noetic Sciences in 1973. The term 'noetic' refers to our inner world and our ability to tune into information not limited by space and time. In other words, our inner psychic.

Mitchell died in 2016. To this day, a team of leading noetic scientists, whom I've had the privilege to collaborate with over the years, continues to use the power of science to investigate our inner space, understanding that both subjective knowing and objective examination are essential for a more complete understanding of the mystery of who we are.

Here's an Earth-shattering notion: Mitchell actually put his feet on the moon, but what felt more awesome to him was his journey within, his experience of transcendent interconnection. There is such a deep message here, that the adventure and sense of meaning and purpose we tend to seek out there really aren't out there at all. They're already within.

HOW TO USE THIS BOOK

Empower your Inner Psychic is an illuminating and comprehensive guide to your inner space. You will learn how to fully utilize the limitless possibilities within you and break through into unseen dimensions. In the process, you'll discover how awareness of your inner world utterly transforms and connects you deeply to your outer world.

It is divided into three parts: the introduction; your inner psychic empowerment programme; and the conclusion.

The introduction explores the science of your innate psychic abilities and offers essential insight you urgently need to reflect on *before* beginning your incredible voyage within.

Your inner psychic empowerment programme forms the main part of this book. It will hand you the keys to unlocking the power of your inner psychic in ways that are optimum to you. It is arranged into seven lessons. Each lesson will offer science-based guidance, along with a series of recommended rituals tailored to the theme of each lesson.

The conclusion and resources sections drill down on all that you have discovered about yourself and reveal further insights and connections for you to seek out moving forward.

The optimum way to use this book is to first read the introduction mindfully and ponder the deep feelings it inspires within you. Then work at your own pace through the seven lessons and have a go at all the accompanying practices. Once all seven lessons are completed, be sure to read the conclusion before proactively checking out the resources, as there are insights for you there too, along with details about how to get in touch with me and claim a free gift.

USE IT

~~~~~~~~~~~~~~~~~~~~~~~~~~

Yes, psychic powers are baffling and their invisible nature makes them hard to explain, prove or define. But why should that matter? Life itself is an unexplained mystery that you simply accept without resistance. So, from this moment on, rather than second-guessing, perhaps you might try accepting and listening to the calm and clear voice within you instead.

And with NASA releasing never before seen, utterly breathtaking images of space in far greater detail than we've ever experienced, in July 2022 just as this book was being completed, and modern science suggesting our thoughts are made of the same energy as galaxies and stars, the infinite potential of your inner space synchronicity is being clearly revealed.

When Thomas Edison, who invented the light bulb, was asked if he could explain and define electricity, because there was a lot of fear and misunderstanding about something that was life-changing but invisible, he is believed to have succinctly replied, 'Electricity is – use it.'

In much the same way, your inner psychic is – use it.

PART ONE

Introduction

'Everyone who wills can hear the inner voice. It is within everyone.'
Gandhi

INTRODUCTION

In is the Only Way Out

Empower your Inner Psychic will prove to you once and for all that you live in a psychic world and you are a natural-born psychic. All you have to decide is what to do with the infinite possibilities within you.

Fasten your seatbelts. It's going to be an unexpected but utterly thrilling inside-out ride!

HIGH TIME

You deserve to feel empowered. You deserve to live a joyful life. Your inner psychic has always known that. It really is high time you did too.

I want to start by reassuring you that your inner psychic is real, very much alive and wanting to break down the self-limiting door of fear that has prevented it from empowering you.

Let's plunge right in with some preliminary revelations. They will instantly boost your confidence in the existence of your inner psychic, by making it crystal clear that any conversation about embracing the psychic within you and connecting to the unseen energies around you is not 'woo-woo', but rooted in the world of science. All those outdated myths about 'psychic ability' will be dispelled too, so that your logical mind doesn't immediately try to shut down or sabotage your inner psychic launch.

THE MAJORITY REPORT

Many of us have had an inner psychic experience already – a dream coming true, an inexplicable hunch, noticing coincidences, sensing the future, just knowing something to be true, and so on. It may surprise you to learn that belief in unseen powers is sharply on the rise and those who think they can on occasion accurately sense things beyond time, space and the material may actually form a majority.[1] Today, all the indications from researchers and scientists are that psychic experiences may well be the norm,[2] rather than the exception.

My mission (and my passion) is to help mainstream the fact[3] that psychic abilities are far more everyday than any of us realize. We all have the potential to activate our innate inner psychic.

But what if you are in the minority and don't think you have ever experienced anything psychic? Even more reason to embrace your inner psychic.

When the brains of people who say they have not experienced anything psychic are studied,[4] it seems that the right hemisphere, or the parts of the brain most associated with insight and creativity, don't light up in the same way as those of people who are more open to psychic experiences do. But when these rare non-psychic individuals follow a simple course of meditation and other psychic development tools, those brain parts start lighting up with great intensity.

In summary, whether you have experienced anything psychic or not, or believe in it or not, you already have psychic potential; you just need to know how to recognize and work productively with your innate sixth sense. And a daily programme of meditation, combined with other simple practices, which we'll come to later, can certainly help you to do that. For now, let's begin by opening your mind.

PERFECT BEGINNINGS

'You must trust yourself.
Trust your own strength.'

Gandalf, *Lord of the Rings*

This book is designed to foster complete trust in the innate psychic potential within you. In time, I hope you will awaken to the enlightening idea that this superpower is in fact the real you.

Don't worry at this stage if you feel sceptical, just open your mind[5] to the possibility that you might just have more creative potential than you think. That's the perfect starting-point for your inner psychic adventure, because psychic growth is strongly linked to levels of self-trust.

Self-belief and psychic development really do go hand in hand. Indeed, low self-esteem is the most common barrier not just to psychic development but to happiness. It took me decades – far too long – to learn how entangled they were, so I hope this book will help you get this sooner rather than later. It's a book I wish I could have read many moons ago. It would have saved me a great deal of heartbreak. But then again, perhaps I needed to hit brick wall after brick wall so I could one day advise with the benefit of hindsight and an intimate understanding of just how painful the struggle to believe in yourself can be.

ONLY YOU

Every time you wonder if there is meaning or purpose to your life, whether you realize it or not, your inner psychic is calling your name. It is calling you to focus on your own ability to look within for guidance rather than constantly seeking validation from outside yourself in material things, relationships, work or through the approval of others. It is also urging you to ditch comparisons with others. The only person to compare yourself with is the person you were yesterday. It's all about your relationship with yourself. Finding inner harmony is your ultimate success.

Real psychic development is all about empowering *yourself* from the inside out. It simply can't be bought, or facilitated by someone else. It has to come from within you. You weren't born to follow or copy others. You were born to be yourself. If there is an afterlife – and after all the decades of research[6] I've done into near-death experiences, I'm convinced there is – and you look back and review your life, you'll find it's not how diligently you followed or copied others that matters, however fine their example. What matters is how true you were to yourself.

Once you understand that you don't need the approval or validation of others to feel whole, and your relationship with your inner world is the key, it is the most liberating and empowering feeling. Things don't get to you in the same way. The expectations and opinions of others don't define you anymore. You are free. You are strong.

You were born an utterly unique miracle of DNA. Your inner psychic works best when you fully believe in your own unique ability to sense what is in your own best interests and make wise and self-loving choices. In the wise words of Jung, 'The shoe that fits one person, pinches another. There is no recipe for living that suits all cases.'

So, in that spirit of essential self-awareness, the sooner you begin freeing yourself from the recipes and expectations of others or the urge to follow or copy rather than forge your own path less travelled, the sooner you'll connect to your extraordinary inner world.

TO YOUR OWN INFINITY AND BEYOND!

I've condensed my decades of psychic world research[7] into this book. I'm confident that it offers all the signposts you need to awaken and develop your psychic powers and live an extraordinary life. Peppered throughout this entire book, you will find that there are references to related studies and other research, including episodes of my podcast *White Shores* that you can listen to as you work through this book, because all of them can deepen your understanding.

White Shores launched in 2019 as a showcase to promote the groundbreaking work of scientists researching consciousness. (If you are wondering about the title, it references the unseen lands in *Lord of the Rings*.) I had no idea how beloved it would become. It is now a platform not just for scientists researching psychic abilities, but also for authentic voices, experiencers, authors and practitioners. It's an entirely free resource and I hope you will take advantage of it as you digest this book. Be aware that the suggested episodes span from September 2019, when *White Shores* launched, to October 2022, when this book was completed, but new *White Shores* episodes will continue to be released for you in 2022, 2023 and beyond.

For your reference, the specific notes that link to a relevant *White Shores* episode are all highlighted in bold. And if you do decide to listen along, be sure to take note of the date of publication of each episode. A strong theme of this book is learning and growing, with life being more about the learning experience than the destination. With an awareness of the date of the episode's publication, you can follow my own progress, both as a podcaster and as a spiritual being, making mistakes along the way but always learning something wonderfully illuminating from every *White Shores* expert guest.

Talking of learning, if you are concerned that the psychic empowerment techniques suggested in this book are time-consuming and complicated, rest assured neither is the case. They don't require oceans of time or any equipment or expensive accessories. They just need you. They are fun too! I hope discovering just how mysterious and magical you are makes you smile. Joy is a vital ingredient in the success of this training programme. If it doesn't make you feel better about yourself, you aren't going to be motivated to stick with it.

It's not rocket science either. It's a condensation of ancient wisdom and optimum research, presented in the form of easy-to-follow daily practices. It's laying down a secure and safe foundation from which you can launch yourself to your own infinity and beyond.

The programme is flexible rather than written in stone. As you work through it and soak up the knowledge, be sure to *personalize* it. Indeed, the more you personalize the techniques, the more effective they will be for you.

So, are you ready to set off on the most amazing journey of your life – the journey within?

DON'T GET USED TO IT!

Throughout this book I will mainly be using the term 'inner psychic' to describe your innate potential to sense beyond your five senses of sight, hearing, touch, taste, and smell the 'psychic' part of you that knows what reason and logic suggest *can't* be known and allows you to mentally time travel beyond space and time. You could call this your consciousness or even your soul. Indeed, the word 'psychic' comes from *psyche*, meaning 'soul' – what is unseen, non-physical and infinite within you.

Sure, this inner psychic draws on what you have experienced and learned already in the material world, but it is bigger than observation, memory and stored knowledge. It is an innate awareness of unexplained sensations that can offer you important guidance. It opens the lines of communication between your body and your mind and offers you a glimpse of your soul. It is a mysterious awareness or hunch – that vague feeling you can't explain, that instinctive response, or that first impression that is subsequently verified. It's that internal radar that scans the world around you. This internal radar is typically surprisingly accurate, even though most of us ignore it or have forgotten how to recognize it and interpret its findings.

You feel uneasy around someone you have just met for no reason, and a few months later, your suspicion that they can't be trusted is confirmed. Sound familiar? This is your inner psychic watching over you. In familiar settings, this sensing instinct often fades or goes silent, but in new settings or when you meet someone new, it is reactivated.

People tell you not to worry if you are a little on edge in new circumstances, because 'you will get used to it in time'. But you don't want to get used to it! You want your inner psychic to stay alert and always be ready to inform and inspire you.

And contrary to what you may think, science is increasingly on your inner psychic's defence case, showing that your hunches – or your irrational ability to sense things that can't be seen or known logically – is innate and entirely natural. It is part of who you are.

Exhibit A is recent research into highly sensitive personality traits.

BORN SENSITIVE

Scientists and psychologists use the term 'sensory perception sensitivity' to describe sensitive personality traits such as empathy, creativity and intuition. All of these fuel your inner psychic abilities.

Studies[8] show that around 20 per cent of people identify as highly sensitive. This means they live their lives constantly sensing what they can't see or explain. The remaining 80 per cent aren't a lost psychic cause, however. Quite the contrary. They can still experience moments of heightened awareness, because research[9] indicates that we are all born with sensitive potential hardwired into our genes.

It seems there is a spectrum of sensitivity, with some of us further along the spectrum than others. However, even the toughest among us, whom others might label 'insensitive', will still experience times in their lives when their innate sensitivity is activated. Typically, this happens during times of great stress and change. Perhaps you can think of a challenging time when your emotions felt close to the surface and impacted your decisions and actions.

Sensitive traits, such as intuition and empathy, likely evolved because they were important for our survival, with intuition helping us pick up on invisible dangers or threats and empathy encouraging us to take care of one another. It also seems that high sensitivity is a genetic trait, in that it tends to run in families, but whether you identify as or are born highly sensitive or not, the big point is that the potential for sensitivity is right there, even if it's hidden deep within you.

Sure, those who are highly sensitive will, of course, find tuning into their inner world more instinctive. But if you don't identify as highly sensitive, this isn't necessarily a disadvantage. The challenge for highly sensitive individuals is to set boundaries to limit over-whelm and to filter out what is relevant from the endless stream of invisible messages flooding in. The challenge for those who are less naturally sensitive is to learn how to open their psychic eyes in the first place. But the upside of being less highly sensitive is that when you do finally learn how to open your psychic eyes, the messages you receive tend to be much clearer.

Rest assured, wherever you may lie on the spectrum of sensitiv-ity,[10] your inner psychic is ready and willing to work with you.

NORMAL OR SUPERNORMAL?

So, with science suggesting that psychic potential lies within us all and it is possible for us all to activate and access it, how does science explain where these mysterious abilities come from and what their nature is?

Quantum physics, the investigation into sub-atomic particles, indicates that everything is made up of vibrating energy strands connected by force fields to form the material world. This means that everything you see and experience in your life, including your invisible thoughts, feelings and senses, consists of the same source material, which is energy.

The way this source energy operates may appear illogical from a rational perspective. Take the concept of entrainment, for instance, which is when the movements of objects vibrating at different frequencies somehow end up synching and vibrating at the same frequency if placed close together. Then there is the even crazier phenomenon called entanglement.[11] Physicists have demonstrated that when sub-atomic particles become entangled, even when they are separated, they remain entangled and somehow continue to act in unison even when no longer close together in distance or time. The physics term for the theory that there may be no such thing as space and locality is 'non-locality'. And if that wasn't strange enough, research[12] has also shown that the observer may be able to influence how energy operates.

Strange science indeed – and I could discuss the Big Bang theory here, which suggests that the universe erupted from a single point of infinite entanglement, or the superstring theory, which suggests that all matter and energy can communicate sub-atomically – but all you really need to know is that from a quantum scientist's perspective, everything, whether visible, conscious and material or invisible, unconscious and 'psychic', is interconnected energy.

This offers a theory or explanation for psychic abilities and the powerful link between your thoughts and your life. It also proposes that psychic senses are simply the result of natural physics, an infinite energy or vibration that we have yet to fully understand.

Quantum physics is a library of books in itself, one that should be written by a scientist, rather than a theologian and mystic like myself, but it does show that psychic abilities aren't just super-normal, they are an entirely natural result of the laws of physics. Your inner psychic both consists of and connects you to the source energy or infinite energy that encapsulates everything that exists within and around you.

And ironically, developing your inner world connects you more strongly to the invisible energies in the world around you. Concentrating on your own personal and psychic growth makes you less rather than more self-centred. You understand that what is within you is also all around you and that you are part of something so much greater than yourself. It's empowering and humbling at the same time. And if that sounds like an oxymoron, get used to it, because embracing the power of opposites and contradictions is part of the mystery to be found on your inner psychic journey.

INTO THE LIGHT!

Near-death experiences (NDEs) may shed some light on the nature of this source energy that exists within and around you. Breathtaking narratives[13] from people who have technically 'died' – meaning their brain and heart have stopped functioning – and then been brought back to life consistently refer to a feeling of energetic interconnection with everyone and everything that they experienced on the 'other side'. They use words such as 'oneness' and 'unconditional love' to describe their experience, suggesting that the source energy we are connected to by our psychic abilities is a blissful one.

NDEs are becoming increasingly common because of advances in resuscitation techniques. Until recently, these people would have died and taken their golden stories[14] with them, but today their experiences are the subject of scientific scrutiny. Some impressive recent studies[15] even point to their potential validity. This is hugely exciting, because it could one day offer proof that consciousness – your inner psychic or the unseen energy of your thoughts, feelings and dreams – can potentially exist separate from your body and brain.

There's a long way to go yet, but what is clear from all this pioneering research into consciousness is that the gap between science and spirit is fast disappearing. Many scientists are becoming accustomed to the idea that inner consciousness matters and we are energetic beings having a human experience.

Indeed, we are both unique expressions and part of an energy source or consciousness that is infinitely expansive. Like drops in an ocean, we are individual and collective at the same time.

MIND THE GAP

A few decades ago, scientists exclusively studied what was observed, material, conscious and tangible. They simply wouldn't have acknowledged the existence of an inner or unconscious world, or the transformative power of what is unseen in our lives, or the idea that everything – including our thoughts and feelings – is interconnected energy, or to put it in popular terminology, 'vibes'. But today there really is a steadily growing understanding of the reality and power of what is non-physical, unconscious and unseen and how it creates and shapes our lives.

That's why throughout your inner psychic empowerment programme, the revolutionary spirit of this bold emerging science will be referenced whenever appropriate. This science cuts right through prejudice and fear and can take us to a better understanding of who we truly are.

I predict that this brave new science of consciousness, so often hidden in academic journals and shrouded by jargon, but simplified and mainstreamed here, will take your breath away.

'ILLOGICAL, CAPTAIN!'

Now that you know science is investigating psychic abilities seriously and you have innate psychic potential, let's change gear. What are *your* thoughts about psychic abilities?

When you hear the word 'psychic', what do you think of? Colourful characters talking to crystal balls or someone charismatic standing on a stage with a headset on, offering messages from beyond the grave? And among all these associations, there's a good chance the term *con artist* may surface.

If the words 'con artist' or 'fraud' do pass through your mind, even for a fleeting moment, congratulations. Questioning what you see, being open-minded, considering all points of view, even ones that make you feel uncomfortable, and looking for the truth beneath the surface is essential for nurturing your inner psychic.

Einstein once said, 'The important thing is not to stop questioning.' As you work through this book, please keep on questioning. Be like Spock in *Star Trek* or Scully in *The X Files* – remain sceptical and question everything.

Questions are infinitely more powerful for your psychic empowerment than so-called factual answers, because they encourage you to reach out and learn new information, whereas answers can lead to complacency. Questions stretch your mind; answers don't. But understand that there can be many different answers to one question!

One of the best things about becoming more psychic is that even when you get satisfying answers, you still go on discovering new things about yourself and the world around you. You need never feel bored again when you begin your inner psychic adventure. You understand that your life is a work in progress, and constantly learning and adding to your store of knowledge is what gives your life deep purpose and meaning.

A PSYCHIC BY ANY OTHER NAME

There are, of course, many words you can use to describe your inner psychic and its expressions: 'sixth sense', 'gut instinct', 'precognition', 'hunch', 'sensitivity', 'clairvoyance', 'telepathy', 'aura', 'higher self', 'manifesting', 'vibrations', 'consciousness', 'spirit', 'soul', 'source', 'vibes', and so on and on. All these already speak to something deep within you, and although they have subtle variations, in essence they are all one and the same, and inter-changeable in this book. They are your inner psychic by another name.

'Extra-sensory perception' (ESP), is a term you may be familiar with. I am not a fan of it because the word 'extra' suggests that it is something additional or supplemental rather than an innate sense. I much prefer 'sixth sense'. For the same reason I am not a fan of the term 'supernatural'. I prefer 'supernormal'.

Channelling, the ability to access information and energy not limited by time and space, is another way to describe your inner psychic (*see page 172*).

But you may well simply settle on 'intuition'. 'Intuition' is a word that is considered more socially acceptable than 'psychic', as it doesn't have the same metaphysical associations. Intuition is associated with insight, instinct or pattern recognition, whereas psychic information is more esoteric, but both surface from the same energy source that defines everyone and everything.

There's plenty of exciting research[16] into intuition and how it is an effective decision-maker.[17] Many of the world's movers and shakers in science, business,[18] art and innovation frequently acknowledge that their intuition has been the vital ingredient in their success. They often describe it as a calm inner voice or invisible insight, using phrases like 'I just knew' or 'My gut told me' or 'I had a hunch' or 'I took a leap of faith' or 'I had a light bulb or *Eureka* moment' and so on.

Psychologist Carl Jung called intuition one of the four functions of the mind, along with thinking, feeling and sensation, and learning how to balance these functions helps us make better life decisions. In his runaway bestseller *Blink*, Malcolm Gladwell calls intuition 'the power of thinking without thinking' or insight that is informed by, but not made by, your rational mind. It is an unconscious understanding beyond reason, logic and experience. Again, what all these scientists, experiencers and experts are really talking about is simply their inner psychic at work.

In summary, whatever word you feel most comfortable using for it, when it comes to a definition, your inner psychic is the infinite aspect of you that is deeply self-aware, feels interconnected to everyone and everything and, if you listen to it, can help you make the best judgements and find the greatest creative inspiration. It offers a wealth of precious wisdom about yourself, your life, your relationships and the situations you encounter, and it may even offer you glimpses of your future or the afterlife. It isn't a total authority or even a moral compass, but it does provide an accurate reading of what is right for you and what is in your best interests.

SETTING YOUR RECORD STRAIGHT

It's important at this very early stage of your inner awakening to ditch some common misconceptions or myths about psychic ability. Clinging on to any of them will stall or completely shut down your psychic growth.

It's for the gullible

There is a false narrative, often promoted by books and movies, that anyone drawn to the psychic world is gullible and lacking in self-esteem. This could not be further from the truth. As the world rebuilds itself after the pandemic, sensitive traits like empathy are emerging as the 'new strong', proving you can be sensitive *and* empowered.

Indeed, low self-esteem is a massive psychic roadblock. Studies[19] suggest that when self-esteem is low, intuition and the ability to make positive decisions take a hit. It seems that anxiety short circuits the brain's associating processes. In simple terms, the higher your self-esteem, the clearer your inner voice will be.

It's for the chosen few

Yes, psychic abilities are a gift, but as has been made clear previously, they are not a gift reserved for the chosen few. Sensitive traits are a gift everyone is blessed with. So, you just need to find your own unique way to activate and trust your inner psychic.

Every time you think of psychic ability as something reserved for the gifted few, you are damaging your self-esteem by promoting the false belief that others are more special than you are. And every time your self-esteem takes a knock, your inner psychic falls down.

It's not real

Just because you can't see something doesn't mean it's not real. You may ignore insights you can't rationally explain because you have been conditioned to dismiss them as coincidence or imagination. Intuition, however, is neither imagination nor random – we all clearly possess intuitive ability in ways unique to each one of us, without exception.

And while we're here, psychic abilities aren't a trick or con either. They are clear insights from within that only serve our highest good.

It's dangerous

Psychic abilities are simply not dangerous. They are not to be feared. They are not a form of mind control. It *is* damaging that over the centuries they have been wrongly associated with the occult, but the big clue is in the term 'inner psychic'! It is the psychic in *you*, so you are always the one in control of it. And should you ever try to use your inner psychic powers for unethical purposes, rest assured this will completely backfire. The psychic vibes you put out are the ones you get back.

It's triggered by trauma

And let's dispel the notion – again fostered by horror movies – that psychic powers can only be unlocked by a terrible accident, crisis or near-death experience. Psychic awakening *can* occur during times of trauma, as a crisis forces us to reassess our priorities, but you really don't need to go through trauma to awaken your inner psychic. Awakening can happen spontaneously, especially during meditation or in a state of flow, when you are immersed in the present moment or task in hand. Again, *you* are in control of when and how to awaken your abilities, no matter what the circumstances or what your age or life experience.

It's anti-religion

Psychic empowerment speaks to those who are spiritual but not religious, but there is no contradiction in embracing your intuition if you are religious. Indeed, many of the world's religions use spiritual terms such as 'soul', 'conscience', 'spirit', 'dream' and so on for what is effectively your inner psychic.

It's overwhelming

You may be concerned that when you start awakening your inner psychic you won't be able to tune out and will feel utterly overwhelmed or drained by all the impressions that flood in. This isn't the case. Again, this is an undermining belief that diminishes and places you in the role of passive victim. But you are in control, remember. You are the one who decides when to tune in and when to tune out. You are the one who decides whether to believe in such 'superstitious nonsense' or not.

It's hard work

Psychic empowerment isn't complicated and doesn't require intense training. You don't need to go to a monastery or retreat or set aside hours of time. Psychic empowerment isn't hard work. If it feels like hard work, you aren't actually doing psychic work.

The 'no pain, no gain' route to success is one many of us have been indoctrinated in, along with a competitive 'survival of the fittest' mentality. But the most beautiful thing about psychic empowerment is that not only do you let go of the idea of struggle – because you learn to trust that your inner psychic will guide you – but you also let go of a competitive mentality. If someone else succeeds, you don't feel envy or that your chances are limited, because you know source energy is infinite and there is always enough success to go around.

It's self-centred

Your inner psychic development will require you to think about yourself all the time and in the process become more self-sufficient. But this isn't selfish, because every time you empower your inner psychic, you also empower your empathy and compassion. Being kind becomes your natural state. And your kindness comes from a position of inner strength, not weakness, making you a real force for good. In short, 'selfishly' concentrating on your psychic development is the most unselfish, egoless thing you can ever do. In the spiritual wisdom of embracing opposites, you understand you are both everything and nothing at the same time.

PRECIOUS PSYCHIC SECRETS

Now that we've dispelled some energy-draining myths, here are some extremely powerful psychic secrets to take their place. Use them as inspiration to reinforce self-belief. Some will take longer to remember and live by than others, and if that's the case, don't worry, because working through the inner psychic programme will reinforce them all, but the sooner you make them a part of the psychic being you are, the better.

Initiate the solution

Empowered by the scientific understanding that your inner world consists of the same energy as the world outside you, and that energy has the mysterious ability to synchronize, be aware that what you focus on in your inner world may attract similar vibrations into your life. *So, give more energy to your dreams and hopes than to your problems and fears.* That's when your life will start to change for the better. And that's why there is an emphasis on positivity, gratitude, adaptability and progression in this book, rather than problems, issues, grudges and roadblocks.

You're likely to have heard about the Law of Attraction, and although positive thinking isn't enough in itself (you really do need to match your intentions with your daily actions), if you want to change your life for the better, there can be no better place to start than with all those conversations you have with yourself. If the only material you give your inner psychic to work with are 'issues', don't be surprised if those start to magnify in your life. Focus on what you actually want to attract instead and notice how much better you instantly feel about yourself and your life.

Be humble

Psychic empowerment is closely linked to self-belief, but self-belief isn't to be confused with self-importance, narcissism[20] or arrogance. This may surprise you – as you will discover, psychic development is all about constantly surprising yourself – but in the general scheme of things, you are really not that important. The world doesn't revolve around you, and other people are typically far more concerned about what is going on in their lives than in yours.

Instead of feeling disempowered by this realization, let it liberate you. Let it help you take yourself a little less seriously. Let it bring a much-needed sense of perspective and lightness of spirit, so you can rise above, see the bigger picture and focus on what truly matters to you.

Other people are not your problem

Of course you want to be loved and approved of. Of course you want to help and inspire others and do what you can to make the world a better place. But at the end of the day, your inner psychic can't make everyone love or even like you, just as it can't save someone from themselves. With the exception of vulnerable children or dependants in your care, what others think about you or decide to do with their lives is not your problem or your responsibility.

Do more nothing

Trying too hard to be psychic will decrease your chances of success. It means you are operating from a place of fear and low confidence, which are both enemies of psychic growth. So, don't strain, force or beg your inner psychic. Let your self-belief and joy in the present moment – rather than making joy dependent on some future outcome – empower you from the inside out.

Although positive daily action is essential, doing nothing sometimes is key too. Trust and the ability to let your mind wander replenish your inner psychic and help it do what it loves to do best – simply attract happiness into your life.

Nothing is final

Once you tune into the idea that everything is energy and energy is infinite, you understand that nothing is ever final, perhaps even death if, as near-death experiences suggest, the energy or consciousness within you carries on. However challenging things get, they will always pass. Every shadow, even darkness, must pass. New outcomes and possibilities are always there on the horizon, waiting for you to believe in and manifest them.

Intuition will arrive from nowhere

One of the best indications that your inner psychic is speaking to you is that an insight comes out of nowhere. It surprises and motivates you, feels unusual and teaches you something brand new about yourself or your life that you didn't know before. It also spurs you from reflection into action. You can't explain it, but you just know what you need to do. Whenever that happens, don't over-analyse it. Simply celebrate and listen to it.

It will just feel right

Another vital indicator that you are in tune with your inner psychic is that you will feel more alive, empowered and on purpose. There will be a calm sense of ease and flow.

By contrast, when you feel drained, directionless and alone, you are still looking outside yourself – to others or to some distant goal – for a sense of worthiness. To get back on track, turn within. Until you can listen to your inner psychic's voice and feel the worthiness within, happiness will elude you.

Accept the challenge

As long as you are alive there will be challenges to deal with. Don't get mad at yourself or feel like a victim. Don't beat yourself up when you make mistakes. Be kind and supportive to yourself. You are always going to be a work in progress and mistakes are essential for you to learn and grow, so instead of fighting against the challenge, accept it. Think of rejection, for example, as protection, a blessed call from your inner psychic that it is time for you to evolve some more. Something better is waiting for you. Understand that *success is never found in your comfort zone*, and when you feel wretched, it is a loving sign from your inner psychic that you are off-course. You need to learn from the difficult experience and grow wiser. It's high time for you to evolve, because you are ready. An inner shift needs to occur. You are being called to do the most wonderful and meaningful thing – upgrade.

Embrace the shadow

There's a shadow side to us all, just as there is night and there is day. The word 'joy' would not have any meaning if it were not balanced by sadness. Don't try to repress or deny the potential for negativity, because it is there within you. Instead, face it, as it will offer you the greatest lessons, and overcoming inner conflict will offer the greatest self-confidence. What you fear the most is where you will grow the most.

Then, armed with the knowledge that you have the potential for toxic behaviour within you, choose to do the right thing. That is true inner strength and where your inner psychic gets its power: knowing you have the capacity for evil, but having the self-awareness, compassion, character and courage to choose the positive.

Love yourself no matter what

If you can love yourself even when you mess up, your inner psychic will flourish. When negative thoughts come in, observe them but don't identify with them. Instead, choose to focus on what is loving and positive within and around you. Know that all emotions are transient. Just because you feel something doesn't mean it needs to define you or will last forever. You are not your thoughts and feelings. They will pass.

Satisfaction, not destination, is your goal

Once you understand that you are more than a physical being, you are liberated. Life just gets easier. Material goals give you a direction and opportunities to learn and evolve, but they don't define you or dictate your happiness anymore. You change what you can and let go of any expectation to control what you cannot change. And when you feel helpless, frustrated or directionless, you know it is because your connection with your inner being has been lost, so you must go inwards to recalibrate.

Living in alignment with your inner psychic and feeling joy right here and right now – not in some conditional future – becomes true satisfaction and the only living path that matters.

Believe it before you see it

We are taught to believe when we see, but your inner psychic defies expectation and often works outside the box, or even backwards. Trusting in yourself *first* and believing that good things are coming your way is how you will help it attract good vibes into your life. You'll see it when you believe it *first*.

Our brains may actually have a default negative and anxious setting, which likely dates back to ancient times when we needed to constantly expect danger to stay alert and alive. But today there aren't typically predators around every corner, so we need to consciously choose positivity again and again to reshape our brains towards this success-attracting positivity. Remember, there is a link between anxiety and low self-esteem and diminished intuition. If you eat something and it makes you feel sick, you aren't going to choose to eat it again and again. It's the same with your thoughts – chose nutritious and delicious ones. And should you struggle to do this, a great tip is to remember a time in your life when you did feel good about yourself. Relive those feel-good feelings, because feelings come before thoughts. Let your mind know this is your new emotional and mental comfort zone.

Questions are your answers

Doubt and fear aren't your enemies, though. They are your teachers – signs that you need to seek new solutions. Too much certainty won't empower you, and remember: progress just isn't made in your comfort zone. The sooner you become comfortable with ambiguity, embrace opposites, face fears, just do your best and let go of the need to know and control everything, and start loving the spirit of adventure that questions can bring, the happier you will feel. In the words of Jung, 'Life is crazy and meaningful at once.'

Success and a happy life are not the same thing

Surprised? But you can be an unhappy success and a happy person who does not appear outwardly to be a success. Obviously, material wealth and recognition can certainly contribute to your happiness in the form of material comfort, but if there is no inner depth to match outward show, you will feel empty. That's why using your psychic abilities *can* help you win the lottery (*do check out my conversation with Powerball winner Tim Schultz*[21] *about his precognitive dream on page 149*), but doesn't typically.

Your inner psychic is far more concerned with your inner wealth and matching the energy of your inner world with the blissful vibration of source energy.

Change yourself first

Too many problems are created in the world by people who haven't seen to their internal needs, so before helping others or trying to change the world, work on your inner healing first. There's a reason why you are asked to put your own oxygen mask on first before helping others in aircraft safety.

As mentioned previously, this isn't selfish or self-absorbed. It is essential. Working on your own inner healing so you can help others from a position of strength rather than weakness actually helps heal the world. Just one person triumphing in a chosen field opens the barriers for others. There was a time when no one could run the four-minute mile, but when that barrier was smashed by Roger Bannister in 1954, others swiftly followed. It's the same for psychic growth. Your personal triumphs and inner growth create an energetic vibration that inspires others to do the same, contributing to the collective.

You aren't here to be everything to everyone. You are here to be there for yourself. And the more you empower your inner psychic, the more your empathy and compassion grow, because you sense how interconnected we all are. You still love, help and encourage others – and advise if they ask – but you don't let their responses or decisions or feelings derail you because you know that what they choose to do is always up to them, just as what you choose to do is up to you.

Rumi expressed this 'change yourself first' rule far better than I can:

'Yesterday I was clever, so I wanted to change the world. Today I am wise, so I am changing myself.'

Let go

You simply can't force your psychic abilities. All that you can really do is learn to notice and trust them. If you have a problem, ask your inner psychic for insight, but if nothing comes through immediately, let go. Trust that insights will come when you are ready. Illumination may appear after a good night's sleep or when you are immersed in another activity. Your inner psychic loves to work in this undercover way when you are distracted or your mind is wandering.

This letting go is often the trickiest part of connecting to your inner psychic, especially when you want something badly, but it's liberating when you get the hang of it.

Trust in yourself

All these precious psychic secrets will lead you towards ultimate self-belief, which, as you've seen, is interchangeable with your psychic development; indeed, it is essential for it.

Chances are up to this point in your life your focus has been on the material – on your job, your money, your social life, and so on – but if your inner life has been neglected, this can lead to feelings of loss, dependency, addiction, fatigue, emptiness and sadness. Indeed, unexplained feelings of sadness, perhaps even depression, can have roots in a disempowered inner psychic.

Remember, whenever you feel low, your inner psychic is calling your name. It is a loving sign that you are off-track and need to redirect from outside in to inside out.

Your inner world – your feelings, thoughts, dreams, memories – is who you truly are. Placing your trust in externals – the material world, other people and things – to bring your life meaning can never make you feel whole. Your relationship with your inner world is the source of all joy and meaning in your life, but sadly, most of us are programmed to look outside ourselves for what only can be found within. We pay more attention to curating our social media presence than to nurturing and empowering our inner world. Where is the sense in that? Let's start redirecting all that self-limiting energy right here, right now.

Let's create a shift NOW.

Take a moment to tune into the beating of your heart. As you listen to its steady beat, celebrate the living miracle you are. It is magic that you are simply alive, with the ability to choose your next thought, feeling and action. Yes, you can *choose* how you react, what you think and how you feel. You don't have to watch your life unfold like a helpless bystander. When you make that simple inner shift, you realize that you have inner strength and a rich inner world to explore. You also discover just how sacred and potentially transformative every single moment of your life is.

Here's another instant fix you can do anytime, anywhere, to remind yourself of your inner power:

Ask yourself if you want to feel empowered or a victim, happy or sad, alive or trapped. Give yourself that very simple choice. Just knowing from within what the obvious answer is going to be – of course you want to feel empowered, joyful and liberated – immediately aligns you with the vision of your inner psychic and the energy source direction you need to be heading in. You give yourself an instant uplift, a moment to commit to a happier version of yourself.

From now on

From this moment on, ask *yourself* as often as you can what the meaning of your life is, and if what you are doing right now makes you feel alive.

Knowing you are responsible for finding meaning and joy in every present moment can feel daunting at first, as of course you've been conditioned to ask others or to look outside yourself, but let go and trust your inner psychic will be there to guide you.

Resistance is futile

Much of what you will uncover in this book will challenge you and ask you to rethink. You may well find yourself resisting and dismissing certain things, but that is why I defer to science as often as I can, because it will reassure you that resistance is futile. *You are an energetic, psychic, spiritual being having a human experience.* You just need to drop your resistance to change, open your mind and heart to infinite possibilities and start living as you've never lived before.

Sure, there will be setbacks ahead, but everything you experience from now on will teach you something valuable. Experiment wildly, love fiercely, trust and hope rebelliously and remember the destination is the direction and not the goal. The goal is the journey – both what it teaches you and the enjoyment of the ride and the adventure of life itself.

Think of it this way: try to imagine *Harry Potter* without the unravelling of Voldemort, or *Lord of the Rings* without the journey to Mordor. It's the challenges, the setbacks, the facing of fears, all that edge-of-the-seat stuff, that keeps you engaged.

Every single day

This is a lot to take on board at this early stage, but don't worry, as everything will be fully reinforced by the daily practices in your upcoming seven-week programme.

Just a quick word about those practices before you leap into them: you will notice that they involve both conscious intentions *and* actions, a merging of your inner and outer worlds. This is because personal growth, whether there is a psychic element or not, begins with what you repeatedly think and also with what you do each day. Studies[22] show that your brain is as much shaped by your daily actions as by your thoughts. In short, although the focus of this book is from the inside out, your outer actions must match your inner intentions.

There's a Japanese proverb, 'The day you decide to do it is your lucky day,' and that sums up the guidelines ahead. You are strongly advised to decide to do these practices every single day until they become part of your life and who you are. There is tremendous power in daily repetition, as long as that repetitive action is done with conscious intention or filled with understanding. In other words, *ritualized*. I'd like you to think of all the recommended practices as your new daily rituals.

Rituals are your friends

Rituals are universal and for everyone, and you don't need to be religious to perform them.

Rituals are not habits. There is a big difference. Habits are unconscious things you do repeatedly, and many may be damaging to your well-being. Rituals are also things you do repeatedly, but you do them with intent, and you are fully aware of the empowering reason why you are doing them. And the reason you are being asked to do them here is because they will help you trust completely in your inner psychic.

If you've ever been for a brisk walk and felt more positive afterwards, that's exactly how the rituals in this book work. The power lies in doing them consistently and how they focus your concentration on the action and, over time, reshape negative-leaning neuropathways in your brain. You may feel that many of the inner psychic empowerment rituals in this book feel small, trivial even, but you will find that repeating them daily has a transformative impact.

Research[23] backs up the life-changing power of ritual. And that change starts with your small daily actions.

Future forward

The big question is: are you going to trust your inner psychic or let it remain dormant? I'm confident you will choose the former, but if you need any more motivation, here's a glimpse of your future with your inner psychic empowered:

You feel energetic, creative and empowered and know there is so much more to you than meets the eye. You make the best life choices and strive to be the best you can be. You are a speedy and effective decision-maker. You know how to avoid problems and sense situations with accuracy. You are laughing more, living your dreams and sometimes even glimpsing the future. Your relationships are thriving too, as you read the people in your life better. Above all, you wake up every morning with motivation, live each day on purpose and retire at night with a feeling of deep satisfaction.

This future forward isn't science fantasy, it's science fact, and can become your everyday reality. As you progress with this book, you will become acutely aware that your inner psychic is more powerful than you ever dreamed. Here's a taster of what lies ahead.

SEVEN LESSONS

There are seven lessons waiting for you. In numerology (*see page 251*), seven is the number associated with the energy of wholeness and good luck, so let the energy vibration of this sacred number flow through you.

Lesson (Week) One: Psyche Yourself Out

Identify the ways you can seek answers from the unknown and discover your psychic signature. Create the optimum receptive mindset with an understanding of some key scientific research and let everyday rituals begin to prove to you that your inner psychic is real.

Lesson (Week) Two: Manifestations

Discover the life-changing power of meditation and manifestation, along with more proven and easy-to-do rituals designed to awaken your inner psychic.

Lesson (Week) Three: Touch your Heart

Use the power of daily ritual to tune into your gut instinct, protect your boundaries and listen to the intuitive wisdom of your body.

Lesson (Week) Four: What Dreams May Come

Understand the science of dreams as a portal to psychic awakening and the ability to glimpse the future, not just in your sleep but when you are wide awake. Practise daily rituals with your eyes wide open and wide shut.

Lesson (Week) Five: Psychic Notes

Explore your natural ability to sense atmospheres and situations, read people and auras, experience the blissful flow state and listen to your inner voice. Allow rituals to unlock these psychic potentials.

Lesson (Week) Six: Become your Own Oracle

Use common psychic self-help tools, such as astrology, to understand yourself, others and your life better.

Lesson (Week) Seven: Become your Own Medium

Learn what science has uncovered so far about the possibility of an afterlife and how personal afterlife rituals can help you continue your relationship with departed loved ones in spirit.

You are advised to work through the lessons in numerical order, perhaps a lesson a week, but if your intuition pulls you towards starting with a specific lesson first or working through the lessons more quickly, listen to it. Just be sure to ultimately progress through all seven lessons, as although each is a totally immersive universe in its own right, they are interconnected. The insights and guidelines in each work best in synergy with the others.

Stay tuned in

And when you've completed all seven lessons, stay tuned in for the conclusion and resources. You'll find more guidance there on the optimum ways to use your psychic abilities in everyday life, a list of helpful organizations and useful reading, plus details about how to get in touch with me if you have any psychic questions, insights and experiences you want to share. (Hearing from readers is what I love best about being a psychic world author, so don't hesitate to reach out.)

And remember, moving forward, that your inner psychic empowerment programme links via references to relevant episodes of my *White Shores* podcast, so you can deepen your understanding of the psychic themes, research and stories being covered.

FIRST LOOK

Now, with all the necessary preliminaries and previews covered, you are officially cleared for take-off. The scene is set, the process is in motion. You are here at last, ready to embark on the greatest adventure of your life.

To mark this sacred moment, try this mini-meditation now. It will only take a few seconds, but it will introduce you to the astonishing space within you.

- Find somewhere safe and quiet. Whether sitting or standing, make sure your posture is good and you have lengthened your spine.
- Take a deep breath, close your eyes and, *keeping your eyes closed*, move your eyes down so they are looking down to the floor.
- Then, with your eyes still closed, imagine your eyes continue turning until they are actually looking right inside you for the first time.
- Whatever you see there, even if it is nothing, send feelings of gratitude to your inner world for a few moments. Trust that your inner world will reveal itself when you are ready.
- Then, after a few moments, bring your closed eyes back from looking down to looking directly ahead.
- Then open your eyes.
- Now smile as broadly as you can and take this clear inner vision with you. Know that you already have the power to see with your inner eyes and that you can attract true joy and meaning into your life any time you want.

PART TWO

Your Inner Psychic Empowerment Programme

'You can never cross the ocean unless you have the courage to lose sight of the shore.'
Columbus

LESSON ONE

Psyche Yourself Out

Your inner psychic potential is an entirely natural manifestation of both your biology and the laws of physics. Sensitivity to what is unseen is encoded in your DNA.[1] Being super alert to potential predators was once a matter of life and death, but due to the advance of industrialization and technology, we have forgotten how to use it. Also encoded within your DNA is an instinct[2] that you are part of something far greater than yourself.

Your task then is not to seek out your inner psychic, but the inner barriers that you have built up against it. To dissolve those barriers and trust that psychic again.

This first lesson will help you cultivate a receptive mindset conducive to empowering your inner psychic. Let's begin by showcasing doubt-dispelling scientific research.

PARANORMAL PROFESSORS

The old-fashioned notion that psychic ability isn't real lingers on and it can create an almighty sceptical barrier. Time to blow it away for good.

Do you know that an increasing number of universities and institutions have dedicated parapsychology units, where psychic ability is researched as a social science and/or a natural ability? For example, the Koestler Parapsychology Unit at the University of

Edinburgh and the Centre for the Study of Anomalous Psychological Processes at the University of Northampton.

Tried and tested scientific procedures are used in these research units, of which the Ganzfeld protocol is perhaps the best known. This completely limits external stimulation and sensory input in experiments so that the subject only has their inner psychic to reference.

Over the years, meta-analysis of research conducted using the Ganzfeld[3] protocol has shown beyond statistical probability (the scientific term for 'chance') that extra-sensory perception exists. For example, research[4] on pairs of people isolated from one another using Ganzfeld protocol to test for the existence of mind-reading (telepathy) has been repeated many times, yielding successful results.[5]

Gary Schwartz,[6] Professor of Psychology at the University of Arizona, has used established scientific protocols to study consciousness, psychics and paranormal abilities. Some of his studies have shown that psychic ability statistically outperforms chance.

The Division of Perceptual Studies[7] at the University of Virginia researches memories of previous lives. Yes, that's reincarnation. Reincarnation[8] stories offer potential indication of survival of consciousness after death. A pioneer in the scientific evaluation of reincarnation[9] who collated compelling stories of past-life recall, many of them from children, was University of Virginia professor Dr Ian Stevenson.[10]

Dr Sam Parnia, Director of Resuscitation Research at Stony Brook University, New York, published a seminal 2014 near-death experience study[11] in the journal *Resuscitation*. This study triggered ongoing research into what happens when we die and the possibility of consciousness surviving death.

Dr Daryl Bem from Cornell University also studied psychic ability using strict scientific and social science mechanisms. His research,[12] published in the *Journal of Personality and Social Psychology*, suggests the reality of psychic ability, beyond chance.

And Dr Jessica Utts, Professor of Statistics at the University of California and President of the American Statistical Association, is on record[13] as saying in her presidential address to thousands of statisticians from all over the world that precognition (sensing the future) seems to work. She stated that the supporting data was strong statistically and if it pertained to something more mundane, it would be more widely embraced. She pleaded to scientists to stop rejecting the data and research in this area because, contrary to popular belief, psychic abilities do not contradict what is already known by science.

From the mid-1970s until 1995 the US government invested time and money in psychic research. Project Stargate was formed to see if remote viewers (*see page 160*) could be used to gain intelligence about America's enemies. The files have all been declassified and although they do show some success, they have been heavily criticized as coincidence. Fear of what can't be seen or fully explained remains engrained. Those scientists who took part in it, however, disagree.

And in 2014,[14] the US Navy allocated millions of dollars to research into the workings of intuition, or 'spidey sense', as they like to call it, as a potential life-saver for members of the armed forces. Here's a convincing quote from the Office of Naval Research:

> Research in human pattern recognition and decision making suggests that there is a sixth sense, through which humans can detect and act on unique patterns without consciously and intentionally analysing them.

In 2021, research[15] led by Lore Thaler, PhD, associate professor at Durham University, suggested that people could tap into their innate sixth sense and learn how to navigate through darkness when eyesight couldn't help.

Much research is focused on intuition[16] and is increasingly showing that it trumps logic time and time again. Those who rely on their intuition are capable of making better, faster and more beneficial decisions. 'Deliberation without attention', according to one study,[17] produces better results than logic, and an increasing number of other respected investigations[18] also indicate that intuition is our best resource. It seems that when the conscious or logical mind is distracted and intuition given free rein, test subjects achieve better results than when they pay full attention or rely on logic. For example, a university medical centre investigation[19] found that when images expressing fear were flashed too quickly for subjects to consciously see them, their brains still displayed anxiety, suggesting that our brains have an intuitive sense of what is unseen.

In another study,[20] when women were asked to eat intuitively rather than make deliberate or pre-planned food choices, they lost more weight than those who went on a diet. This suggests that we may know our own bodies better than we realize. Indeed, research[21] led by neuroscientist Dr Julia Mossbridge[22] and parapsychologist Dr Dean Radin[23] indicates that our bodies intuitively know things before they happen, sending us signs like increased heart rate or sweating to warn or guide us. This is called presentiment or predictive anticipatory activity. It's significant, as it indicates that psychic senses should not be considered superior to physical senses, but that they should work together.

In addition, there is research[24] spearheaded by NSW University neuroscientist Professor Joel Pearson which shows that intuition is not imagination but a scientifically provable impulse that can be enhanced with practice.

And then there is also compelling psychological research based on a five-year study[25] and published in 2022 in *Spirituality in Clinical Practice*, which suggests that psychic experiences are real, are fast becoming the norm, not the exception, and should be taken seriously by mental health professionals.

So, alongside revolutionary paranormal investigation in universities and growing awareness among psychologists that psychic experiences are real, the science of intuition – the acceptable face of your inner psychic – is alive and thriving. Proving to you, and anyone willing to pay attention to it, that evidence of your innate psychic ability isn't just anecdotal. It's real.

INDEPENDENT RESEARCH

There are also several remarkable independent organizations that conduct their own science-based experiments and research psychic ability and how people experience it. Some publish their findings in leading scientific and academic journals.

THE INSTITUTE OF NOETIC SCIENCES (IONS)

A team of leading IONS scientists, which includes bestselling authors Dr Helané Wahbeh[26] and Dr Dean Radin,[27] EEG technology pioneer Dr Arnaud Delorme,[28] Dr Loren Carpenter[29] (who as well as being a physicist just happens to be a double Oscar-winner) and Dr Garret Yount[30] (who just happens to be the inspiration for the protagonist in Dan Brown's *The Lost Symbol*), are conducting on-going studies[31] that show paranormal experiences at the very least deserve scientific investigation, as people have reported them from the beginning of time and continue to do so. They are part of the human experience and need to be treated as data, and what the IONS team are finding is that when studied scientifically, in the large majority of cases there is every reason to believe the explanation is paranormal. The IONS channelling research programme spearheaded by Dr Wahbeh,[32] for instance, has been consistently demonstrating that some channels can receive verifiable information they could not have access to otherwise. Through researching channelling, IONS hope to learn more about how consciousness can transcend human experience.

IONS is currently leading the world in consciousness research,[33] but they are by no means alone in their quest. There are other notable organizations out there seriously investigating psychic abilities. To name a few:

THE SOCIETY FOR PSYCHICAL RESEARCH (SPR)

Founded in 1882 the SPR was the first organization to conduct scholarly research into human experiences that challenge contemporary scientific models.

THE WINDBRIDGE INSTITUTE LLC

Launched in 2008, the Windbridge Institute[34] is dedicated to conducting world-class research on mediumship[35] and phenomena currently unexplained within traditional scientific disciplines.

Windbridge are currently pioneering research[36] into the genetic traits of professional mediums and psychics. Indications are that psychic abilities run in families, but other unusual common factors have been identified, such as being non-heterosexual, being left-handed, having an autoimmune disorder, and experiencing childhood trauma.

THE RHINE RESEARCH CENTER

This research centre advances the science of parapsychology[37] and fosters a community for individuals with an interest in the paranormal. Research carried out over a number of decades does point in the direction of psychic abilities being real, with some of Rhine's volunteer psychics accurately guessing symbols on unseen cards with an accuracy score twice what statistic chance would have given.

THE GALILEO COMMISSION

Led by David Lorimer[38] and a project of the Scientific and Medical Network, the Galileo Commission's remit is to open public discourse and find ways to expand science so that it can accommodate and explore human experiences and questions that it is currently unable to integrate.

MAKING SENSE

~~~~~~~~~~~~~~~~~~~~~~~~~~~~

The recent movement towards legitimate scientific investigation of psychic phenomena has elevated the subject beyond the merely anecdotal and closer than ever before to natural and demonstrable fact. Combine that with the surge of interest in the inner world that the recent pandemic and the lockdown dream[39] phenomenon unleashed, and it is becoming increasingly difficult to entirely dismiss the reality and life-changing potential of the inner world.

Not forgetting that some brilliant Nobel Prize-winning scientists, past and present, such as Professor Brian Josephson, Alan Turing, Max Planck and Wolfgang Pauli, to name but a few, have been very open-minded about the paranormal.

However, despite these promising signs, there is no denying that definitive proof of psychic ability isn't there yet. In addition, the sad abundance of fraudulent psychics[40] challenging credibility, lingering myths about psychic ability and a lack of proper funding for research make it easy to understand why there is still a long way to go.

The important thing for you to accept, though, is that progress *is* being made by credible researchers all over the world. Whenever scepticism creeps in (and it will), return here to remind yourself of that steady progress. You may want to take an interest in that research, or even volunteer to be a part of it, as there is no telling what it may uncover in years to come. Either way, rest assured that the spirit of that research pervades and informs your inner psychic empowerment programme.

HOW YOU PERCEIVE

And at the same time as science is pushing the boundaries, even though organized religion[41] is on the decline, more and more ordinary people[42] are opening their minds to the reality of what is unseen. The steady rise of modern mysticism is encouraging, but far more progress could be made if more people actually understood *how* psychic information is perceived.

The truth is your inner psychic is deeply subtle and elusive, and that's why many of us fail to pick up on it. We don't notice it, or if we do, we confuse it with an over-active imagination. However, the more you recognize your inner psychic and focus your attention on it, the louder its voice becomes. It's like a muscle – the more you use it, the stronger it gets.

That's why how you can recognize psychic insight is what you are going to discover first. As always, expect the unexpected. You go about your day, and when you least expect it, there's no knowing how your inner psychic might reach out to you.

Whenever you see, hear, taste, touch and smell, you are tuning into or responding to energy vibrations created by your five physical senses. Your psychic or sixth sense works in exactly the same way, the only difference being that it works with energies that can't be seen or rationally explained. But this lack of explanation shouldn't demotivate you. Every day of your life you trust in invisible energies you can't explain, from electricity to sound waves to love. Psychic energy is no different.

Remember, you yourself are unexplained energy. Scientists don't know why you think and dream, for example, but every day you think and every night you dream. So, given that your entire life is a wonderful mystery, your psychic ability is just another part of it.

Understanding how you can perceive psychic information is crucial, because if you don't understand how it is revealing itself to you, then you just won't notice it. Most of us wrongly think that psychic messages come externally, as a blinding vision or disembodied voice for example, but that is rarely the case. True psychic power is an *inside-out job*.

And the subtleness of this inner voice is its power. It forces you to focus and reflect deeply on the hidden meanings beneath the material, or what ego, logic and reason have not taken into consideration. We live in such a noisy, restless world today. There isn't a person alive whose life would not benefit from a little more reflection.

YOUR FANTASTIC FOUR

Your inner psychic speaks in countless ways, but for the purpose of clarity here are the main categories that you need to be aware of. There is a lot of cross-over between the categories and infinite sub-categories, but these really are, in my humble opinion, the fantastic four. I'll illustrate each with a striking example:

Psychic seeing, AKA clairvoyance (the seer)

You may notice visible energies (auras) around people (*see page 169*), but psychic seeing typically manifests when your eyes are closed and images unfold in your mind's eye. If you are thinking this sounds a lot like daydreaming or visualization, you are correct. Daydreams and internal visual images are your inner psychic at work. You also see with your psychic eyes every single night in your dreams. (*Lesson Four covers psychic seeing.*)

127 Hours

This movie dramatizes the true story of American outdoorsman Aron Lee Ralston, who survived a canyoneering accident by cutting off his arm. He was trapped between two rocks and as he felt his life ebbing away, he had a vision in his mind's eye of his future son playing. This vision gave him the strength to amputate his own arm. A few years later, he got married and had a son, whom he recognized as the son he had 'met' in his vision.

Psychic hearing, AKA clairaudience (the oracle)

This is inner sound. It is when you can't get a word, phrase, sound, quote, conversation, voice or song out of your head. Sometimes overhearing music, or sounds, conversations or songs in the material world can trigger meaningful connections too. (*Lesson Five covers psychic hearing.*)

Gandhi's 'still small voice'

Mahatma Gandhi, the father of Indian independence, often spoke of a voice that guided him. He called this 'the still small voice', and for him, this inner voice and the voice of God or consciousness and truth were one. In his own words: 'What I heard was like a voice from afar and yet quite near. It was unmistakable as some human voice definitely speaking to me and irresistible. I was not dreaming the time I heard the voice. The hearing of the voice was preceded by a terrific struggle within me. Suddenly, the voice came upon me. I listened, made certain it was the voice and the struggle ceased. I was calm.'

Psychic feeling, AKA clairsentience (the sensor)

This is when your body does the talking. It is your gut feeling expressing itself through unexplained kinaesthetic sensations like a fluttering stomach, a dry mouth, nausea, an itch, increased heart rate or sweating. Or perhaps a sense that someone is staring at you or you are floating on air. It is also a heightened sensitivity to things you touch, taste or smell and the ability to feel or sense 'vibes' or atmospheres or what others are feeling. (*Lesson Three covers psychic feeling.*)

Iced tea[43]
US army officer Sergeant Craig Hendricks was in the joint international task force in Baghdad. He was in an air-conditioned trailer, but experienced a compulsion to go and drink iced tea, even though the trailer had cold water and he never drank iced tea. Initially, he dismissed the unusual compulsion, but it became so persistent that he eventually decided to take a break and walk outside in the searing heat to get an iced tea. About a minute after he left his trailer, a rocket struck close by which would have likely killed him.

Psychic knowing, AKA claircognizance (the knower)

This is a simple inner knowing. You could call it 'resolve'. It's those times in your life when you don't know why, but you just know what you need to do next, or what the outcome of something is going to be, or when something is going to happen, or what someone will say or do. (*Lesson Five covers psychic knowing.*)

James Dean

In 1977, actor Sir Alec Guinness was interviewed by British broadcasting legend Michael Parkinson. In the interview (which you can watch on YouTube), he shared that in 1955 he had randomly encountered the young actor James Dean in a restaurant. He had never met him before, but Dean recognized and approached him, and the two actors started chatting. Dean told Guinness he was very excited, as he had just bought a new Porsche. He took him outside to show him the car, which still had a bow tied around it. As soon as Guinness saw the car, he inexplicably knew without any doubt that if Dean drove that Porsche, he would be dead within a week. He told him what he sensed, but it fell on deaf ears. Exactly a week later Dean died in a car crash while driving his new Porsche.

YOUR PSYCHIC SIGNATURE

You concentrate when you want to hear something more clearly. You narrow your eyes when you want to see something in the distance. You already have a wonderful ability to focus and concentrate your physical senses – whether they be hearing, seeing, touching, tasting, or smelling – when you want to pay closer attention.

You can do exactly the same with your inner psychic: you can learn to consciously focus your attention on the way it is trying to talk to you.

You want to empower all your psychic potential – and should stay open to any way psychic information reveals itself to you – but you may well find as you work through the lessons in this book that one or two ways feel more natural to you than others. This is your unique psychic signature.

Be aware that your psychic senses can, on rare occasions, give information to you through what you encounter in the material world, but it's far more likely to be an internal experience. And even if you experience an external clue, it will ignite an inner sensation.

GETTING TO KNOW YOURSELF

For the following foundation rituals, and indeed all the rituals in this book, pay close attention to your psychic signature. How is psychic information coming through to you? Let the following questions guide you:

⊙ Are the psychic impressions you receive visual? Do you see them unfold in your mind's eye or in your dreams? Are you a seer?

⊙ Are you highly receptive to sounds – both those you hear externally and those you hear internally? Are you an oracle?

⊙ Do you pick up 'vibes' or feelings? Are you a sensor?

⊙ Do you often just know things but have no idea why? Are you a knower?

Over time, as mentioned earlier, you may find that you have one or two preferred ways to receive psychic insight. This is useful information because focusing on an area of psychic development that doesn't flow as naturally to you is going to block your progress. For example, if you are someone who simply can't visualize, there's no point forcing yourself to do endless visualizations.

TAKING NOTE

As you progress through the seven lessons, be sure to keep a record of any psychic impressions in a dedicated blank notebook or journal and, if you can, identify how they came through to you. Sometimes you may not be entirely sure how you received the insight, as there is a lot of cross-over between psychic reception areas, so don't worry if that's the case. Just feel grateful that your inner psychic is awakening.[44]

Do date stamp any psychic impressions. Describe them as fully as you can. Like a detective, you are going to gather your own evidence or personal proof that you are psychic. Keeping a psychic journal, diary, document or record is a great learning tool, especially when you look back on it with the benefit of hindsight.

Chances are any impressions you perceive will be faint, especially as you start to do these psychic empowerment rituals, but this subtlety is no reason to discount them. The more you discount them, the weaker they become, and the more attention you pay to your sixth sense, the stronger it will become.

EXPLANATIONS AND ESSENTIALS

All the foundation rituals in this lesson begin with an explanation of why you are being asked to do them. Understanding why you are doing a ritual is essential for its success because you will then perform it with mindful intention.

The explanation is then followed by simple instructions to help you bring that ritual to life.

Make sure you perform your foundation psychic rituals in solitude (unless the ritual suggests otherwise) and in a calm and relaxed manner. Then after the ritual you need to ground yourself.

These three essentials – solitude, calmness and grounding – do need to accompany each ritual moving forward. Here's why:

Your quiet place

Your psychic empowerment training is private and between you and you alone. Make sure you carve out some quiet for yourself each day, where you won't be disturbed or distracted. It doesn't have to be acres of time, around fifteen minutes a day is ideal, but even if you can only spare a few minutes, that can work.

If you live in a busy household, this may mean getting up before anyone else or deliberately choosing to retire somewhere where you can be alone. You need to switch from focusing on what is going on around you to what is going on within you, and the best way to do that is to be alone, away from other people and distractions.

Calm centre

Stress blocks messages from your inner psychic. So you need to find the best way to relax before you perform your rituals. That's coming up next because it is so fundamental. Lesson Two explores the calming impact of meditation and connecting with your breathing, but there are other ways to chill. You can listen to your favourite music, take a warm bath, write in your journal or make a cup of herbal tea with honey. My favourite way to relax is to give myself a hand massage with rose-scented hand cream.

Grounding

Empowering your inner psychic connects you to a higher reality, so to avoid feeling spaced out, be sure to ground yourself and reconnect to the physical world after each ritual. Grounding simply means doing something practical, like having a glass of water, stretching and yawning, stamping your feet, or eating a piece of fruit.

Writing your impressions down in your psychic empowerment journal is also a great grounding exercise. Remember, your psychic empowerment journal – a blank notebook or file you write in – is one day going to become your proof that you are a natural-born psychic.

FOUNDATION RITUALS

The rituals in this first lesson lay the foundation for all the inner work you will be doing moving forward. Aim to make them part of each day from now on. Underlying them all is the theme of moving your awareness from out there to in here.

Ritual: First things first

Make the first fifteen to thirty minutes of your day screen free.

WHY?

If the first thing you do each morning is reach for your phone, the message you are sending your inner psychic is that the needs of others or what is happening in the external world are more important than your internal growth.

Being held hostage by your mobile, screens and social media, as many of us are today, silences[45] your inner psychic, not to mention your cognition, creativity and sense of self-worth.

Your best insights will come when you are offline rather than online. Although you can be creative on your phone, the great majority of the time you are passively consuming rather than living your life. Your intuition can't be nourished by a screen or the online ramblings of others. It is nourished by what you think, feel, dream and do for yourself away from screens.

Being unplugged for the first thirty or so minutes of your day will dramatically kick-start your intuition. The first thirty minutes dictates the tone of the day, as your brain is waking up then and highly receptive to suggestion. That's why this is the very first ritual you are asked to do, because even if it's the only thing you do, you'll still make significant progress.

HOW?

Before you got to bed at night, switch off your phone, and preferably charge it in another room and not by your bed. If you need to be on call in case something urgent comes up, make sure only essential calls can come through and not all the other unnecessary beeps and alerts.

When you wake up in the morning, instead of automatically reaching for your phone, focus your mind on any dreams you may have had. This immediate focus on your internal world is incredibly liberating for your inner psychic. For years it has been starved of attention and now it is first and foremost! And, like anything in life, the more attention you pay to it, the more it will magnify or reward you.

If you are tempted to check your phone, notice that craving but don't act on it. Simply tell yourself you will check in half an hour or so. Remind yourself that unplugging empowers your creativity and intuition. The only energy that should have control over you is you.

Notice how powerful this simple act of self-control is for connecting to your inner world.

Savour those sacred early morning waking moments. Your brain is super receptive right then, as it is in an impressionable theta brain-wave state. Indeed, the conscious thoughts you have on first waking can reshape your brain, so be sure to fill your mind with thoughts of excitement about the day ahead.

Then, when you get out of bed, do an enormous full-body stretch, complete with battle-cry yawn if you can. Don't minimize yourself. Send a physical message to the universe and your inner psychic that you are expansive. Tell yourself you are good enough.

Continue to keep away from your phone for half an hour if you can. It is very hard to find inner peace when you are a slave to your phone. Ensure your 'get ready for the day ahead' routine also transforms into a sacred ritual by doing everything mindfully.

To connect to your intuition, you need to feel calm and positive. Mindfulness[46] is a great way to do that. This is because living mindfully in the present moment – in other words, giving what you are doing your full attention – occupies your conscious mind with the task in hand and allows your brain's associative intuitive processes to get to work. That's why you may suddenly get inspiration when you are showering or brushing your teeth or doing something that is routine. When your conscious mind is distracted by an activity, your inner psychic roams free.

But whatever you decide to do, make sure you treat your first waking minutes with the respect that they deserve and that your focus is on what is manifesting within you. You may need to get up a little earlier than usual to make sure you get this sacred 'you' time, but it is well worth it. Indeed, many of the world's most successful people are very early risers, describing the peaceful early hours of the morning when they are not distracted as their power time.

ADD ON

The benefits of being away from your screens are so great that you may want to go one step further and start switching off your mobile or taking regular time out from social media later in the day too. Much, of course, depends on your work and how much you need to be online, but as long as you keep those first minutes of your day entirely mobile-free, this is a huge step in the right direction.

To risk repeating myself, your inner psychic struggles to make itself heard when you are constantly distracted by the demands of your phone and multi-tasking.

Ritual: Back to front

Think backwards.

WHY?

Thinking backwards helps you cultivate a mindset receptive to empowering your inner psychic, because your inner psychic doesn't follow the linear, logical or rational laws that govern your everyday life. It belongs to your unconscious world, where there is no sense of order, logic, reason, time or space. You visit this upside-down, infinitely creative world every night in your dreams.

Thinking in backwards order blindsides your logical brain and sends a message to your inner psychic that you are willing to defy logic and hear whatever it has to say to you, not just in your dreams but when you are wide awake too.

HOW?

At the end of each day before you get into bed, spend a minute recalling your day backwards. Start with the present moment and then travel back in time until the moment you woke up and hopefully recalled your dreams.

Sounds easy, but it is anything but. Your logical mind will immediately try to impose order. So, aim for ten-second bursts of backward thinking until you feel more confident. Focus on the main events, like supper, afternoon walk, lunch, morning routine, breakfast, and don't get bogged down in the details.

As always, don't stress or force anything. Simply having a go at this exercise every day really stimulates your mind and your inner psychic will applaud your sincerity.

ADD ON

Anything that encourages you to view life from a new perspective can help wake up your intuition or let it know that you are more receptive to it. So, try writing with your non-dominant hand, taking a different route to work, learning a new language, and so on. Your inner psychic will love your willingness to get comfortable feeling uncomfortable and to experience doing something a different way.

Ritual: Think right

Upgrade your thinking.

WHY?

In your everyday life you typically ensure that what you see, hear, touch, taste or smell is pleasurable. And when that isn't possible, chances are you'll learn from it and do something different next time. For example, if you don't like the taste of a certain dish in a restaurant, you won't order it again. The burnt hand really is the best teacher. So why not do the same with your thoughts? Seek out pleasurable ones rather than constantly repeating ones that hurt you.

Your inner psychic wants you to feel good because it knows that this positive vibration is more likely to inspire you. Research[47] has shown that gratitude is a happiness-attracting magnet. Giving thanks every day is a way to not just cultivate the idea of being a separate inner being capable of witnessing your life, but also of being able to choose what you focus your thoughts on. Every day is your chance to consciously choose gratitude and joy and empower your inner psychic in the process.

HOW?

Every day before you go to bed, make a ritual of thinking about three things that you feel grateful for. They don't have to be big things. They can be as simple as the comfortable bed you are sleeping in or the unconditional love of your pet or the chocolate sprinkles on your cappuccino. Just focus for a few moments on those three things and notice how choosing to upgrade your thoughts in this way instantly elevates your mood.

ADD ON
Another nutrient for your inner psychic is awe. Aim to seek out things that fill you with wonder. Then savour them. Listen to music or watch the sunset or a starry night or a plane taking off. It doesn't matter what you do, just tune into feelings of awe as often as you can.

Ritual: Another level

Start looking beneath and beyond the surface of things.

WHY?
Making unexpected associations is the stuff of genius. It is also the language of your inner psychic. A great work of art captures people's attention because it has so many hidden depths and associations. Your inner psychic wants you to observe the world around you as if it is a great work of art with layers of hidden meaning.

HOW?
Choose an everyday object. It can be anything – an apple, a pencil, a coat – but ideally choose something you can see and have a personal connection with.

Now for a minute or so think about this object on multiple different levels.

First think of your personal associations with that object. For example, if you choose an apple, think about the colour and taste of that specific apple and why you like or dislike apples.

Then move your thoughts to apples in general, all the different types, how they are grown. Think about their history and famous apples, from Newton's demonstration of gravity to Eve's forbidden fruit.

Then think about the purpose of apples. How they are a source of nutrition. Think about being nourished and what the word 'nourishment' means to you.

Then move to apples being a fruit and the symbolism or abstract meaning of fruit. What could an apple be a universal sign or symbol of?

The layers of association can be endless. Don't be afraid to let your mind roam and uncover all sorts of hidden and unexpected links. If the famous Romantic poet William Blake could see the world in a grain of sand or heaven in a wild flower, what can you see in your humble apple? Look for the extraordinary[48] in the ordinary.[49]

ADD ON

Whenever you get a chance in your daily life, look beneath the surface for deeper meaning as well as for more expansive meaning. Stop taking everything you see or experience at face value. Just as you are uncovering a whole new world within you, there is always more beneath the surface of everyone and everything you encounter or experience in your daily life.

Ritual: Your inner psychic handshake

Open up clear and positive communication with your higher self every day or whenever you need reminding of the power within you.

WHY?
Intention is asking your mind to help you do something, and this ritual is going to get your conscious and unconscious mind on your side.

HOW?
Close your eyes and imagine what your inner psychic or unconscious or intuitive self looks like. I always imagine my inner psychic as a flying white unicorn with purple wings, but if you see your inner self as Thor or Wonder Woman or anything or anyone else, however bizarre, that's fine too. Just imagine whatever you feel best represents you.

Now imagine your inner psychic is standing right in front of your conscious self or body. Remind yourself that both your conscious and unconscious selves have essential roles.

Then ask your inner psychic to shake your hand. With your eyes still closed, physically reach out your hand as you ask.

Hopefully your inner psychic will agree, but if it doesn't want to shake your hand, ask it what reassurance it needs before you can work together in harmony. Then give it that reassurance.

Seal your intention to work together for your highest good with an imaginary handshake.

ADD ON

You can shorten this ritual to a simple intention stating that your inner psychic and your conscious self will always work together in harmony.

You can also repeat this exercise and when you shake hands, ask your inner psychic to only show you positive glimpses of your future or what is in your best interests.

FAQ: 'How can you tell the difference between genuine psychic impressions and anxious, negative self-talk?'

☺ Psychic insight empowers you, it won't accuse, criticize, alarm, diminish or demotivate you.

☺ Psychic insight is gentle but persistent. It will keep recurring until you take note.

☺ Psychic insight is typically unexpected, unusual and fresh. It will seem to come out of nowhere and surprise you, whereas ego tends to feel rational, even when it isn't, and recycled.

☺ Psychic insight is vivid, clear, calm and unambiguous. There will be no room for doubt or confusion.

☺ Psychic insight doesn't remain in your head, it encourages you to take positive action.

☺ Psychic insight serves both your own and the greater good.

☺ Psychic insight tends to focus your energy on the present, whereas anxiety is all about what hasn't yet happened.

◉ Psychic insight tends to be felt from your stomach, whereas fear strikes your entire body, raising your heart rate, etc.

◉ Psychic insight proves to be correct over time. (That's why keeping a record of psychic impressions matters.)

SAIL AWAY

~~~~~~~~~~~~~~~~~~~~~~~~~~~~~

Recognizing how you perceive psychic information is a deal-breaker. The lessons that follow will guide you through that receiving and manifesting process.

As you move forward, don't forget to keep on taking notes and keeping a record in your psychic empowerment journal of the impressions, associations or insights that are breaking through, and how you have perceived them.

Are some of the impressions you are recording related to your daily life? Don't worry if they don't make sense right now. Your psychic empowerment journal is always best read with the benefit of hindsight. It's in the days, weeks and months or years ahead that you will start to see a pattern or perhaps even glimpses of your future emerging.

Some of the rituals recommended in future lessons will play to your psychic receptor strengths more than others. Have a go at them, but don't stress if they don't all resonate. You are on an epic voyage of inner discovery. You are a glorious energetic work in progress, and the only way to evolve is to think like a scientist and experiment wildly. Making mistakes will help you learn. Remember Edison and his 1,000 attempts at the light bulb – he learned what didn't work from the 999 before. Imagine if he had given up after attempt three or thirty-three or ninety-nine!

Over time, simply refocus your attention on those rituals that play to your strengths and notice and record any associations and impressions. Then, with an inner smile, look up and prepare to sail away on your next great psychic adventure.

LESSON TWO

Manifestations

Becoming aware of a whole new world within you that is independent of and separate from your body and the sea of sensations flooding in from the material world is psychic awakening.

There are many names for your brave new inner world, but one you may not have considered yet is *you*, the real you.

Hold that thought.

This lesson will focus on two vital 'M' words in your inner psychic empowerment: meditation and manifesting. Fall head over heels in love with them both as soon as you can and your psychic awakening will transform into psychic *becoming*.

MEDITATION

Meditation,[1] or calming and concentrating your mind, sounds deceptively simple but sometimes it can be anything but. Your mind doesn't only have an inbuilt bias towards compelling negativity but also has a tendency towards distraction. Indeed, research[2] shows that our minds wander from the present moment up to 50 per cent of the time. And other research[3] shows that every single time we blink, our brains shift attention.

That's why practising meditation every day is supremely powerful for empowering your inner psychic. It is the ultimate way to focus and concentrate on your inner wisdom.

THE PROMISE

Master basic meditation skills and you are well and truly on your way to unleashing your inner psychic. Not only does meditation activate the creative parts of your brain, it has other proven benefits.[4] It has been shown to reduce stress and anxiety, boost mood and concentration and aid problem-solving. Indeed, some studies[5] promote it being taught in schools, as students who meditate regularly are more likely to graduate.

Studies[6] also indicate that regular meditation can actually change how your mind works and help you deal more calmly with stress. And that's the reason it is so beneficial for your psychic empowerment. Anxiety and poor concentration are major psychic roadblocks.

There is a close bond between intuition and meditation:

- Intuition is the ability to make the right decisions without thoughts distracting you.
- Meditation helps you detach from your thoughts so you can silently connect to your inner guide. From a calm and fully present meditative state of mind you wait patiently and without judgement for solutions to surface from your inner world. You notice or observe whatever images, thoughts, feelings and guidance arise.

SOUNDS GREAT, BUT ...

I'm sure you've got the message. Meditation is the key to your inner psychic empowerment. But what if your mind is constantly preoccupied and meditation doesn't come naturally to you? If that's you, you sound a lot like me.

If there is a meditation course out there, chances are I've been on it. But the more courses I went on, the more frustrated I got. Instead of feeling calm, I felt anxious. I felt I was doing something wrong. If I managed to clear my mind, I'd get so excited that all I could think about was that I had cleared my mind! The calming absence of thought totally eluded me.

It took me far too long to appreciate that my obsession with the end goal of clearing my mind was the problem. What I needed to turn my attention to was the process. It wasn't the absence of thought, it was having the awareness that thoughts were happening without identifying or interacting with them. It wasn't zoning out, it was allowing the present moment, with all its contradictions, to reveal itself and letting go of past tension or future expectation. It was noticing what was happening within in the now.

To repeat, it wasn't controlling or stopping the endless stream of thoughts. It was observing them and either allowing them to meander to their own creative connections or simply watching them flow. Does that help?

TAKE TWO

You are a busy person. The last thing you may want to do is set aside acres of time each day to sit and do nothing. But when you take just two minutes – yes, that really is all you need, forget all that you may have read about it taking hours, who's got time for that? – you aren't doing nothing. You're fuelling your inner psychic.

If the word 'meditation' still feels off-putting, simply think of it as a time to recharge. It doesn't matter what you call it, just find your calm place for a few minutes each day at a time that works best for you. Many people find it optimum to meditate first thing in the morning, while others prefer the evening. Try different times of the day to see what works best for you.

There are a bewildering amount of meditation guides, gurus, apps and systems out there, so experiment if you want, but try to keep your cool. There is no right way to meditate. If you find yourself forcing or straining for results, you are heading off-course. Stop if any tension creeps in and try another time.

Accept that your flow of thoughts will be rapid when you meditate, because you can't turn off your thoughts. But what you can do is turn off your response. Just observe your thoughts without judgement or commentary.

And when your two minutes is up, be sure to congratulate yourself. You may find that you immediately feel refreshed because you have taken time off from the tyranny of your thoughts. You have reminded yourself that what you think doesn't define you and doesn't need to control you. Your thoughts are separate from who you are.

Here are a few effective mini-meditations to incorporate into your day and your life:

Ritual: In and out

Focus on the flow and feel of your breath.

WHY?
Study after study[7] has suggested that deep breathing can relieve stress, boost energy, concentration and the immune system, decrease the risk of insomnia, induce calm and help you feel happier.

Most of us breathe very shallowly and quickly, however deep breathing from the stomach rather than chest is optimum for holistic well-being. Setting aside dedicated time every day to make a conscious effort to breathe deeply is an instant calmer. It also encourages you to breathe deeper more of the time.

HOW?

Set a two-minute timer. Sit somewhere comfortable and quiet with your back straight. You don't have to close your eyes, just slow down your breathing, both your inhalation and your exhalation.

Breathe in from your stomach through your nostrils and breathe out through your mouth. Placing your hand gently on your stomach and watching it rise and fall as your stomach moves can be a way to facilitate tummy breathing. Be sure to completely fill your lungs with each inhale and to completely exhale until there is no breath left.

Now with your mind's eye watch your breath going in and out of your body. Notice the different feeling of the in-breath and out-breath. You can imagine you are breathing in positivity and exhaling anxiety, or you are breathing in light and breathing out fog. Or simply remind yourself that taking time out to breathe deeply boosts your holistic well-being.

When your mind wanders (and it will), just notice that and gently bring your attention back to the flow of your breath.

When the timer goes off, stand up and stretch to ground yourself.

ADD ON

Breathing is something you have to do, so you may as well do it optimally! Every time you take a couple of minutes to simply meditate on your breathing, notice how it helps to ease tension.

If counting to five as you inhale, holding your breath for a count of five and exhaling for a count of five helps your awareness and focus better, go for it.

If peaceful music or ambient sounds or diffusing essential oils that are known to aid meditation, such as lavender and frankincense, help you calm your mind as you dive deep with your breathing, bring it on! You need to find your own deep breathing meditation equation.

Ritual: Just say *'Omm!'*

Repeat a calming mantra.

WHY?

A mantra is simply a single word you say or chant during meditation to keep your mind focused. The sound may evoke certain feelings within you. Chanting has been shown[8] to ease stress, boost concentration and calm the mind, all of which, as you know very well by now, are music to your inner psychic's ears.

Chanting may be associated with religion, but you don't need to be religious to embrace the life-changing power of the calming sound of your own voice.

HOW?

Again, take a few minutes out of your day at a time that works for you. Set a timer for two to five minutes and sit quietly with your eyes closed.

Commonly used mantras are the primordial sound of Omm (pronounced 'Aum') or the soothing sound of shalom (peace) or the comforting sound of 'love' or 'peace', but you can choose or make up any sound or word that evokes a feeling or quality that you want to attract into your life.

Then say the word out loud repeatedly, slowly savouring the sound and the feeling. When your mind wanders (and it will), simply notice that it has wandered and gently bring your attention back to the sound of your own voice.

When the timer is up, open your eyes and feel the energy of the word you have spoken swirling within and all around you. Take it with you back into your life.

ADD ON

You may feel slightly ridiculous when you first try chanting; if so, just tell yourself that it is very similar to humming, which many people do for relaxation. Nobody considers humming odd. And if you like to hum when you shower, walk or meditate, that's great meditation too.

Ritual: Bright eyes

Get your daily nature fix.

WHY?

Science[9] is proving what you intuitively know already: fresh air and green spaces are good for you. Time spent in nature boosts not just your body and mind, but also your intuition. This is because your inner psychic is a vibrant living energy vibration and it responds to living vibrations rather than non-living or human-made ones. So, an optimum place to seek psychic awakening[10] is in the natural world.[11]

HOW?

This is one meditation method that will likely need more than two minutes of your time. But apart from that, a daily walk in a natural outdoor setting where you can focus your attention on appreciating the living wonders that greet you is all that you need. Half an hour or more is optimum, but if you can only spare ten minutes, then make those precious minutes count.

If it isn't possible to find a wood or park, find a green space or garden to walk in, or even a tree to lean against.

If going outdoors isn't an option, open the window, drink in the fresh air and focus all your attention on the natural things out there, even if that's just the breeze.

ADD ON

If you love animals, the more time you spend with your beloved pets[12] or caring for and protecting wild animals,[13] birds, fish, reptiles or insects, the better. The bond[14] between human and creature is forged by your (and their) innate empathy and sensitivity.

Living things have an altogether different energy than non-living. Moving forward, start scanning your living and working environments and whenever you can, get closer to what is natural. Bring plants into your home and work space. Seek out green and blue spaces. Remember that your inner psychic gathers strength from the energy of natural living things. So, give it a daily nature fix.

Ritual: Your eyes have it

Gaze at a mandala.

WHY?

Mandalas are a wonderful meditation aid. These beautiful circular designs reflect how your life fits into the larger circle of life and how your inner and outer selves are interconnected. *Mandala* is a Sanskrit word for 'circle' and refers not to the shape itself but to the circle of life.

HOW?

Use the cover of this book as a mandala. Set a timer for a couple of minutes and study it in detail as if you are going to memorize it. Make it your sole focus.

When your attention wanders (and it will), notice how the circular design has a hypnotic effect and draws your eyes to the centre. Don't struggle against this natural focusing of your eyes. Let it happen.

When the timer goes off, blink several times.

MANIFESTING

Alongside meditation, there's another 'M' word you may have heard a lot about in recent years. Manifesting has been hijacked by modern self-help gurus and celebrity culture, but it isn't a new discovery, it's age old. And neither is it as mysterious as it is often presented to be. It is simple, even logical, once you understand the energetic reason behind it.

Manifesting[15] is just moving your focus from what you don't want in your life – your problems or what you lack – to what you actually *do* want in your life. It is consciously choosing thoughts and feelings that align you with your goals and then watching your dreams come true. It is becoming your own force, getting your mind on your side.

For example, if you want to feel more confident, you think of yourself as being confident already. You don't focus on your lack of confidence. If you want more financial success, you focus your thoughts on feeling wealthy instead of feeling deprived. If you want to feel happy, you focus your thoughts on what you have to be grateful for, not on what you feel you lack. If you want to be loved, you focus on feeling loved already. You adjust your mindset to attract from source energy the life you want.

You may well have heard the story of actor Jim Carey writing himself a cheque for a million dollars *before* he was a famous actor earning millions. Carey was manifesting. He was operating under the assumption that what he wanted to attract into his life was a given. It was a future reality he just needed to attract with the power of his trust and expectation.

Manifesting is making yourself fully aware of your own power to attract and create the life of your dreams. In other words, you really understand what it is that you want and concentrate your emotional energy on that so the law of 'like energy seeks like energy' can get to work. It's psychic empowerment by another name.

If you are thinking this sounds a lot like the power of positive thinking, you're right. It is the Law of Attraction that million-selling books like *The Secret* popularized. As the introduction made clear, there may well be scientific backing for the Law of Attraction, because we live in a universe of interconnected energy. There are also a number of studies[16] which show that affirmations (*see below*), prayer, blessings and gratitude have a healing and life-affirming impact, suggesting that instead of being the last resort during times of personal[17] or collective crisis,[18] perhaps prayers should be the first resort.

As an interesting aside, random number generators (RNGs) are lab instruments used to test whether mental intention can impact random outcomes. This was previously done with dice, but RNGs ensure the events are truly random. Global consciousness[19] or intention research[20] is a worldwide version of an RNG experiment that tests to see the impact of focused attention by large numbers of people at the same time. So far, the results[21] are encouraging.

Manifesting, however, is a form of personal rather than collective prayer. It is connecting you to your infinite potential. It is the language of your inner psychic. The success you want to attract already exists in source energy. Your inner psychic wants you to raise the vibrations of your thoughts and attract into your life the happiness that is your birthright.

Be aware that manifesting is deeper and richer than simply being upbeat or eternally optimistic. You can't dream of achieving success and then sit and watch TV all day. Positive expectations need to be matched by positive actions.[22] You need to walk your talk, otherwise you are one of those frustrating people who are all promises and no actions.

In life you learn to trust and value people for what they actually do, rather than what they say. Manifesting works exactly the same way. It is a psychic law that only helps when you follow through, and your actions are as instrumental in attracting what you want into your life as your thoughts.

Now that you understand how simple but crucial manifesting is for your psychic empowerment work, let's get you started with some intention-setting techniques. The following rituals, indeed every single ritual in this book, must be performed every day from now on with a conscious decision to believe *before* you see.

Ritual: Repeat after me

Repeat positive statements.

WHY?

Your mind believes what you repeatedly tell it with your thoughts. It doesn't actually know the difference between opinion and fact and is extremely suggestible, especially first thing in the morning and last thing at night, when it is in a relaxed theta brain-wave state.

The brains of very young children are mainly in theta, which is why negative messaging to the young is extremely damaging. Those messages quite literally shape their young brains. (The unlived lives of parents and other carers can cause so much damage to children.)

The good news – the empowering news – is that whatever age you are, you can consciously choose to rewire your brain with your repeated thoughts.

And twice a day you have an unmatched opportunity to change your life for the better. A single statement repeated first and last thing to yourself over a period of several weeks has the potential to plant a seed of success-attracting self-belief in your mind, which, if it is nourished with positive action, can manifest into reality.

'Affirmation' is the term used for repeating positive intentions or statements to yourself. An affirmation works by interrupting the negative thought patterns that are blocking you and replacing them with life-affirming ones. They make your thoughts work *with* your inner psychic rather than against you.

Affirmations are typically spoken rather than thought. Saying something out loud and then repeating it out loud several times for emphasis helps your mind see what you are saying as absolute truth, as the words don't just come from your thoughts but also your voice, giving them double power.

Believing what you think and say is a manifesting fundamental, because when there is true belief, you not only attract what you want, but you naturally take action to actually make it happen.

HOW?

First thing in the morning when you wake up and last thing at night when you are about to go to sleep, repeat the following affirmation, or something similar that resonates better with you, out loud three times.

I am the engineer of my own life and my inner psychic attracts limitless happiness and success my way.

If you feel embarrassed doing this because you share a bedroom, you can always do it in the bathroom or somewhere else where you can be alone. The important thing is to say it out loud and proud.

ADD ON

Another powerful morning and evening affirmation you could and should experiment with in the coming days and weeks is:

Positive things are coming my way.

Again, perhaps you feel slightly ridiculous talking out loud to yourself in this upbeat way, or don't think something so simplistic can in fact work. But have you actually tried? Going out of your comfort zone and constantly surprising yourself is what your inner psychic demands of you.

You really, really can change your life by changing your focus, choosing how you think and feel. It's not a cliché to say that if you can dream and believe in it, you can do it.

Ritual: Get ready

A little more contemplation.

WHY?

Letting your mind create its own reality through daydreams (or description if you struggle to form mental pictures) helps keep what you want at the forefront of your mind, so that you are more likely to notice and attract opportunities in your daily life that can help turn it into reality.

Contrary to what you may have been taught at school, daydreaming[23] is most certainly not a waste of time. It may even be the best use of your time, because it fires your intuition and creativity. One study[24] showed that daydreaming when you have a problem can help you solve it, as problem-solving areas of the brain become more active when you are daydreaming.

Mind wandering is often associated with things like laziness or poor attention, but your brain is actually still active when you daydream. And intriguing research[25] indicates that when the brain isn't doing anything in particular, it still functions at a high level – much higher than previously thought.

In short, you could call this contemplation, or even boredom, but whatever you call it, your inner psychic loves it whenever you daydream or think with passion about what you want to attract into your life.

HOW?

As with the majority of your psychic empowerment rituals, find somewhere where you can sit down and feel comfortable and won't be disturbed. If you have a busy timetable, set a timer. Aim to keep the soles of your feet on the ground during this expansive exercise.

Then take a few deep breaths. Imagine you are breathing in calm and exhaling tension.

When you feel centred, create a picture in your mind of what you want to manifest in your life. Keep your eyes wide open as you do this. You are daydreaming.

Don't be an observer of your daydream – place yourself right in the picture. *Feel* how you will feel when you get what you want. It's fine to suspend disbelief. If you've always dreamed of becoming an astronaut, or winning an Oscar or a Nobel Prize, let your mind take you to space or the award ceremony. You can be or do anything – it's your dream boat. You are director, producer, script writer and actor. Let your feelings take you in the direction of your big dreams.

There really are no rules with your daydreaming ritual. As long as you are daydreaming about something you love or which makes you feel great, you're on the right track.

When the timer goes off, retain the confident belief that your dreams of happiness are real and will manifest in your daily life. Let your daydream raise your vibration so that you fully expect good things to come your way.

You may even want to end your daydream by saying out loud the following affirmation:

My dreams often come true. Good things are coming my way.

(You'll notice the word 'often' here. It's there for a reason. In these early stages, the aim is to convince yourself, and adding 'sometimes' or 'often' can make it easier to believe.)

Note: If you can't visualize, please don't let this alarm you. Aphantasia (*see page 123*) is the rare inability to voluntarily create mental imagery and it is more common than is being reported. What you need to do instead is write down or describe out loud the life of your dreams. Indeed, this may even be more powerful than visualization, because your brain jumps to attention when thoughts are written down or verbalized. There's a reason why in a law court swearing out loud on the Bible to tell the truth, the whole truth, and nothing but the truth is treated with such reverence.

ADD ON

The best time to do this ritual is mid-morning or mid-afternoon. Avoid doing it directly after a meal or just before bedtime, as you may feel too sleepy, or first thing on waking, as you need to get on with your day. And if you can, perform it outdoors while walking in a natural setting. Do be sure to look where you're going, though!

Everything starts with a daydream. Read the biographies of great scientists, innovators and artists who have manifested their dreams and you will typically find a sacred tradition of them longing for time to reflect and dream, from Buddha who meditated under a tree to find enlightenment to Thoreau practising solitude in an isolated cabin to perhaps the most famous loner, Einstein, who liked to play his violin and spent more time pondering than working. He once said he concentrated best and was at his most creative when he was 'away from the horrible ringing of the telephone'.

So, if you find yourself craving time to just let your mind wander, you are in very fine company indeed.

Studies suggest that up to 50 per cent of us are introverts who crave more time alone to dream, but even the remaining 50 per cent, the extroverts who derive energy from social situations, can still benefit from a little solo contemplation, just as introverts can benefit from a little socialization. Our culture seems to favour extroverts (introverts are more favoured by Eastern contemplative cultures), but your inner psychic will thrive whenever there is an opportunity for a daydream, regardless of whether you identify as an introvert or not.

Ritual: Write it down

Clarify your goals.

WHY?
Your inner psychic craves positive expectations, but it also passionately longs for clarity, to know what you actually want so it can get to work and point you in the right direction. That's why goal-setting is a manifestation essential.

It reminds you to focus clearly on what you want, not on what you don't want.

And one of the best ways to get clear about your goals is to write them down. It seems that the act of writing things down helps your mind focus and increases your chances of achieving them, perhaps because when you write something down it feels official, like a contract.

Sometimes we don't really know what we think about ourselves and our lives, or even what we really want, until we read what we write.

HOW?

Find a notebook with blank pages in. On the first page of that notebook, write down your life goals. Be specific if you can, but if you can't, it's fine to simply write down that you want to be happy and successful. Don't pressure yourself if you can't think of something immediately. Trust that more specific inspiration will come in time, but if it doesn't, the goal of being a happy person is a beautiful one and a great launch pad.

Then every evening before you go to sleep, write down a few sentences – or more, as this is your journal, so how much you write is up to you – about your day. Don't focus so much on the events, but on how you felt about those events. Focus on what you learned about yourself and, most important of all, whether your actions, thoughts and feelings were aligned to your life goals and what you can do to make tomorrow better and more in tune with your vision. If you prefer to speak into a voice recorder on your phone when you are too busy to write in your journal, that can work too.

Please don't feel you need to be upbeat all the time in your record-setting. And don't beat yourself up if your interests shift and your goals change. The key to evolution is adaptability. Sometimes what worked in the past just won't resonate in the present. Let go and move on.

The power of journaling is in your honesty and ability to learn, adapt and reflect. Remember this is a private conversation between you and your inner psychic. Nobody will see it but you. Save what you want the world to know about you for your social media. For true self-awareness, there is a part of you that must always be kept sacred and private. If you over-share with others, you run the risk of losing yourself in their expectations of you.

Powerful people with a strong sense of purpose and identity have inner strength because there is a part of themselves that they keep private. They don't need validation[26] from others for what they say, think and do. They trust their inner psychic above all others.

ADD ON

When it comes to goal-setting, you may want to wait to focus on your intentions when the moon is dark or new, or when you can barely see her in the sky. The moon influences the tides, and humans are up to 70 per cent water, so living in harmony with the phases of the moon is a way to connect to the natural rhythms and energies of the Earth.

Lunar living[27] has surged in popularity in recent years, with books, courses, rituals and requirements for all the many different phases of the moon. But you don't really need to buy into any of that. Simply knowing the three main phases of the twenty-eight–twenty-nine-day moon cycle – new, waxing to full and waning – will suffice, with the new moon being an ideal time to set intentions; the waxing and full moon the ideal time to take action and initiate; and the waning moon the ideal time to let go, pause, trust and reflect.

It's very easy to find out which phase the moon is currently in by searching online or simply by looking at the sky – is the moon revealing more of herself each night (waxing) or is she diminishing (waning), is she a full circle (full) or barely there at all (new or dark)?

FAQ: 'I'm meditating and manifesting like crazy, but no results. What am I doing wrong?'

Nothing. You are where you need to be right now because there are important things your inner psychic needs you to learn about yourself before you see progress.

For starters, you need to stop looking for immediate results. Looking for an instant fix is like planting a seed and expecting the plant to grow and flower overnight. It takes patience, discipline and positive action, as well as the belief that good things will happen, for your focused intentions and manifestations to align. It also requires a willingness to acknowledge[28] the reality of disadvantages[29] and injustices[30] in the material world and that not everyone has the same privileges as a starting-point. Your inner psychic will help you change what you can, and when you are faced with things you simply can't change, it will empower you by changing how you react to them.

In short, manifesting is swifter and easier for some than others. That's just life. However, once you understand that the destination is not the goal, but feeling empowered independent of whether your hopes have materialized, that's when you allow the power of meditating and manifesting to utterly transform your life. Try not to confuse your inner psychic with external circumstances – treat triumph and disaster just the same. Above all, enjoy the *process* of your ongoing psychic evolution. Repeat after me: *It's about the journey, not the destination.*

Reread the introduction to this book, in particular the psychic secrets. Stop looking for resolution, solutions or the idea that you can only be happy in the future or when certain results happen. Focus instead on your daily thoughts and feelings and whether or not your daily actions are in line with what you want to attract into your life and bringing you joy. If they aren't bringing you joy, why are you still doing them?

And when those pesky setbacks happen (which they will), don't lapse into victim or 'poor me' mode. They are opportunities to learn and grow in experience and life wisdom. If fear takes over, know there is a courageous and detached part of you that can always rise above and look ahead to joyful things. Crisis is opportunity to evolve. And negative feelings are also an opportunity to learn and grow. They are a sign you need to course correct, learn and grow some more and reconnect even more deeply with your inner psychic in the process. The greater the challenge, the greater the potential for growth, and the meaning of our lives is to evolve, so whatever life throws at you, you are living your meaning. In short, there are only lessons and blessings in life.

You don't go to bed at night worrying whether the sun will rise in the morning. You just know it will. The certain belief that even when darkness falls or setbacks happen you will rise again is the direction you always need to be heading towards. This isn't blind optimism or fantasy thinking, it is simply feeling gratitude for or learning from the present and believing in your own future joy.

THERE IS NO TRYING!

Meditation and manifesting need to become part of your daily life.[31] Giving yourself a daily dose of quiet space and time to meditate will both awaken and empower your inner psychic. Remember there is no doing, or trying or thinking at all. You don't try. You don't do. You don't think. You simply observe yourself. Just be.

It's easy to lose track of time when you get the hang of meditating and enter that observant, calm, peaceful state outside your thoughts, which is why your meditation rituals have suggested the use of a timer. You can extend your time to five or ten or more minutes, but remember it's quality, not quantity, that counts.

Make setting your timer a part of the ritual. As you set it, tell yourself (set the intention) that for the next couple of minutes you are going to rise above your thoughts and meet your inner psychic without fear, uncertainty or judgement.

And as far as manifesting is concerned, there is no trying here either. There is only believing and trusting that good things are coming. Performing your manifesting rituals remind you that there is infinite energetic potential within and around you. And when you connect to this higher vibration from the inside out and awaken and empower your inner psychic, you are on fire. You are in a state of psychic flow, attracting only what is in your best interests.

Meditation and manifesting are the secret PIN codes you need to unlock your inner psychic and upgrade your entire life. Don't let another day slip by without their sacred power touching your soul and their supreme wisdom lighting up your life, infusing you with the courage of hope[32] and pointing you in the right direction.

LESSON THREE

Touch your Heart

'I've learned that people will forget what you said, people will forget what you did, but people will never forget how you made them feel.' What Maya Angelou is describing here is the reason why your emotions are the most organic and effortless way for your inner psychic to speak to you. They are also the most obvious and commonly reported (and ignored) psychic sense. Not sure what I'm talking about? Here are some examples:

- ☾ You meet someone new and for reasons you can't understand they make you feel nervous.
- ☾ You suddenly get butterflies in your stomach, along with a feeling of unexplained anticipation.
- ☾ When conversing with people, you can sense their pain even though they may be smiling broadly.
- ☾ You enter a room and sense an atmosphere.

As you have already learned, everything has an energy[1] vibration. Your body is like a receptor which can tune into these vibrations and send you messages about them in the form of feelings. Have you ever heard yourself saying, 'It just doesn't *feel* right!' That's a psychic feeling.

I'm sure you've read incredible tales of mothers sensing something was wrong with their babies and this sixth sense saving the child's life. Or someone sensing when a distant loved one was in danger, even though there was no way they could have known.

Stories[2] of these kinds of invisible encounters[3] never fail to comfort and inspire.

PRESENTIMENT

Your inner psychic feelings typically reveal themselves through physical sensations, such as your hands shaking, or your throat going dry, or you feeling sweaty. Sometimes your entire body may pick up a psychic signal – that is the feeling many of us get that someone is standing behind us or staring at us when actually there is nobody there – but most commonly psychic emotions occur in the stomach or the heart.

You've bound to have felt your heart beating faster or your stomach filling with knots or goosebumps rising for no apparent reason. It's as if your body actually knows something is coming.

This type of psychic feeling is called *presentiment* by scientists.[4] Pioneering investigation[5] shows that a few moments before an unpredictable event occurs, bodily changes (including heart rate, pupil dilation and brain activity) predict that event, indicating that our bodies can sense the future when something significant is about to happen, even if we don't know what that future might be. The scientists involved in this research believe that presentiment is a real physical effect that obeys natural laws – just laws nobody understands fully yet.

The message, both from within and from the world of science, could not be clearer: presentiment is your inner psychic expressing itself through your body, most typically through your gut and through your heart rate.

THINK TWICE

The likes of Steve Jobs, Bill Gates and Richard Branson follow their gut feeling. Einstein said his helped him develop his theory of relativity. Countless scientists, innovators, artists, entrepreneurs, traders and pioneers also reference[6] their gut instinct as the reason for their success both professionally and personally. There's even a study[7] which suggests that gut feelings are the key to success in financial trading.

Your gut is, of course, your stomach area, with the most sensitive points being the abdomen and solar plexus. It's not surprising really that this is a psychic feeling centre, as there's a nervous system matrix there linked to every organ in your body, including your mind and heart, and it helps regulate major bodily functions. The nervous system function of the stomach is so intelligent that scientists have even called it the second brain,[8] and neural tissues in your gut do influence your emotional state. Other research[9] suggests that heeding gut feelings may create neural pathways that enhance the mind–body connection.

So, paying attention to your body talk can quite literally reshape your brain.

All this corresponds with Eastern spirituality, according to which there are energy centres called chakras located at various points in the body, each associated with a certain quality. The stomach area relates to creativity and empathy. It is also believed to be the chakra that connects the physical to the invisible world of spirit. (Bear in mind, though, that although the bodily location is often similar there is a difference, as chakras are centres where energy flows *into* your body but psychic sense receptor areas, such as your stomach, are about energy flowing *from* and through your body.)

Now that you know how super sensitive and clever your stomach is, in the coming days pay attention to all those times you instinctively turn away or towards someone, or cross your arms when you are feeling defensive, or hug a cushion when you feel vulnerable. Your inner psychic is urging caution.

THE POWER OF YOUR BEATING HEART

Your life begins and ends with the beating of your heart, but your heart does more than keep your body and brain alive. In many spiritual traditions, the heart is the source of love, compassion, deep intuitive wisdom and feelings of connectedness.

Everything depends and focuses on your heart, making it the perfect home for your inner psychic. It's not surprising that the best results in paranormal research tend to come from study centres that have nurturing and caring environments or experiments that involve emotional intensity and human interaction. And a defining feature of some of the world's most revered spiritual healers, as well as people with highly sensitive personality[10] traits, is their ability to feel things deeply and spontaneously, and this enhances their creativity, and predisposes them to heightened psychic ability.

Research backs up the wisdom of the heart. Studies[11] from the HeartMath Institute indicate that when you feel peaceful, positive and creative, your heart beats in a calmer way. HeartMath researchers have coined a term for this, 'heart coherence', which means a state when your body, mind and heart are in perfect harmony. It's a deeply aware, almost meditative state which generates intuitive wisdom and calm.

CLEAR FEELINGS

~~~~~~~~~~~~~~~~~~~~~~~~

When we talk about presentiment, gut instinct and heart wisdom, what we're actually referencing is the area of psychic awareness known as clairsentience. I prefer to call it *clear feeling*. This is the ability to sense vibes through bodily sensations, the sense of touch or inexplicable feelings, and either immediately or over time those first impressions tend to be proved right. It may well be the least recognized psychic sense, but it's one that can speak to you loud and clear.

Sky's story:

> I woke up in the middle of night. There was a storm raging outside. My bed was warm and comfortable and my windows shut, but I felt the urge to go to the rest room. It wasn't urgent and I could easily have fallen asleep, but I decided to get up. When I was in the bathroom, I heard this almighty shattering bang. It was like an earthquake. Rushing back into my bedroom, I saw a huge branch from the tree outside my window had smashed through the window, landing on my bed.

Here's a quick way to familiarize yourself with clear feeling:

- Close your eyes and think about your pet or someone you love. Conjure up that person or animal[12] with your emotions. How do they make you feel? What is your body telling you? Do you feel a warm calming glow in your chest area?
- Now do the same for someone you don't love or admire and again notice your feelings and how your body reacts. They will be very different.

Closely associated with this sense of clear feeling are psychic taste, smell and touch.

Psychic taste is when you become aware of tastes or sensations in your mouth but you aren't eating or drinking anything. Always rule out health explanations first, but if there are none, you could be sensing energies with your taste buds. For example, your mouth may go dry or may taste unpleasant when you suspect someone is lying to you.

Psychic smell is similar. It's when you smell something, but when you follow your nose, there is no logical reason for that smell.

Psychic touch or clear touch is when you feel something physically, such as a muscle twitch or dizziness or a tingling sensation and there is no physical stimulus for that sensation. It's presentiment by another name.

Of course, it is important to always rule out any medical reasons with your GP if you are experiencing bodily sensations that are unusual.

ILLOGICAL LOGIC

The following rituals are all carefully curated to help you recognize and interpret your clear feelings. Remember, you aren't going to sense thoughts or images here; you are zeroing in on the world of feelings and physical sensations. Your feelings matter, but you already know that. Think about it: however well-thought out or rational or logical a plan is, if it doesn't feel right to you, it's not worth investing your time or energy in, is it?

Sounds illogical (your inner psychic wouldn't have it any other way), but trusting your feelings, even if common sense dictates otherwise, is actually the reasonable and feasible approach.

Ritual: Body talk

Hear your body.

WHY?
Performing this ritual every day will help you become familiar with the way your body talks to you, so that the next time it happens, you are more likely to notice it.

HOW?
This ritual can be performed at any time of day. You just need a few minutes – set a timer for five minutes if you are pressed for time – and find somewhere where you can be alone and sit or lie down comfortably.

Close your eyes and tell yourself that you are going to focus on how your body feels rather than the stories in your mind. Allow yourself to sense your body as an energy-filled vortex with vibrations swirling within and around you. Gradually slow down your breathing.

Become aware of how fast your heart is beating.

Then focus your attention on your forehead. Many of us wear a constant frown without even realizing. Relax that frown.

Then allow yourself to yawn, and as you do so, become aware of your jaw, cheeks, nose and ears. Sense how they feel.

Then move your attention to your shoulders, arms and hands. If it helps, tense and then relax each body part.

Move to your back and chest, and then shift your focus to your abdomen. Linger there a while before sending your awareness to your legs and feet.

When you have sensed the energy levels of your entire body, remain still and listen. Is any part of your body talking to you? Don't force anything. Just notice what sensations surface and where you feel them. See if any insights or questions accompany those physical feelings. And if some of the sensations have an obvious physical cause, such as dehydration, muscle strain or an upset stomach, resolve to take better care of your body and consult a doctor if need be. But if there is no obvious physical cause for a sensation that feels unusual or short-lived, then it's your inner psychic.

When you are ready, open your eyes, stretch and adjust to your surroundings. Close the ritual with gratitude for this special opportunity to feel and appreciate the wisdom of your body.

ADD ON

Perform these mini body-sensing scans throughout the day. The more often you do so, the more sensitive to bodily feelings and to your environment you will become. Notice any physical sensations before you make a decision or when you meet someone new. Give your body wisdom a chance to be heard.

Even if your gut instinct is perhaps proved wrong, it's important you take note, as there was still a reason your body was trying to tell you something. Perhaps there still is something you need to pick up on, so keep on tuning into your body. It knows what is in your highest interests.

Ritual: Heads or tails

Toss a coin for your inner psychic.

WHY?
The best way to tune into your gut instinct is to keep on testing it. The more you learn how it speaks, the stronger and clearer it will get. That's what you see with great athletes, artists, pilots, and so on. They have tested, practised and trained so much that they are able to anticipate intuitively what will happen.

Though intuition can seem to appear out of nowhere, it is often the result of observation and making inspired connections from stored knowledge. It is dedicated practice and discovering through trial and error when your inner psychic has something to tell you and when it doesn't.

Whatever the situation, your intuition[13] already knows the best decision or way forward for you. It gets to work behind the scenes, making connections from what you already know. When you start thinking rationally – for example, listing pros and cons – without you realizing, it compares your gut instinct with the preference your conscious mind is edging you towards. If your conscious or rational perspective and your intuition agree, you feel calm and certain, but if they don't, you feel anxious and confused.

This ritual encourages you to test your intuition whenever you feel undecided. It gives it a chance to be heard over the voices that often drown it out.

HOW?

You need a coin for this ritual and you also need to be undecided about something in your life and in need of a 'yes' or 'no' answer. That indecision can be a trivial one, for example should you attend an event or not, or something big, like should you move house or not. Ideally, it should be a question where you will, over time, learn what the correct answer is, so that you can see if your intuition ultimately proved to be correct.

In your mind, assign heads as a 'yes' and tails as a 'no'. Hold the coin in your hand and reflect on your dilemma. Ask your inner psychic to give you a clear answer. Then flip the coin.

When you see what the result is, pay close attention to how you feel physically and emotionally. Perform a body scan. What is your gut or body saying? Do you feel physically energized or drained by the result? This is your inner psychic informing you of the right answer. In other words, it is not the result of the coin toss that matters, but your inner psychic's immediate response to that result.

If you feel physically energized by the result, then there's your answer. But if you find yourself wanting to go for two out of three flips to make your final decision, chances are your inner psychic is leaning to the other choice.

Write down your emotional response to this coin flip exercise.

ADD ON

In the coming days, weeks, or however long it takes for the correct answer to reveal itself, refer back to your notes about your physical and emotional response.

If the decision this experiment caused you to make ultimately proves to be wrong, that is still helpful, as it shows you that what you thought was an intuitive response ultimately wasn't. Chances are wishful thinking or anxiety were making the decision for you.

If, however, the decision proves to be right, you'll find it easier to recognize exactly how it feels when your psychic feeling is expressing its wisdom, and you'll be able to connect to it without needing to toss a coin.

Ritual: Traffic lights

Red, amber, green.

WHY?
Feelings are like inner psychic detectives. This ritual is a wonderful alternative to the coin toss exercise above.

HOW?
Set aside five minutes and for about a minute focus your attention on the colour green. You can have the colour in front of you on a card or picture, or you can visualize it in your mind's eye. *Feel* the colour green and every association you have with it. Make a conscious decision that only pleasant associations will go with the colour green.

After a minute, switch your focus to the colour amber or yellow. Look at the sense of possibility it brings, but also the caution and reflection it suggests.

Finally, lose yourself in the colour red and the possibility of excitement but also the danger and putting on the brakes that it suggests.

Then ask yourself a question you want a 'yes' or 'no' answer to and see what colour presents itself to you first.

ADD ON

Practise this exercise lots in your daily life. Whenever you need to make a decision, notice what colour you feel or receive.

Ritual: Water break

Let your energy flow.

WHY?

Dr Masaru Emoto[14] is well known for his water consciousness experiments. He taped positive messages on the bottom of one glass of water and negative ones on the bottom of another and directed loving emotions to the former and negative ones to the latter. Over time, the water exposed to loving emotions created beautiful, ordered crystals, whereas the water exposed to hateful ones created chaotic, ugly ones.

HOW?

You are going to conduct your own Emoto experiment, but not with water. You need two pencils that are exactly the same and two identical paper bags to put them in.

In one bag put a piece of paper with the word 'love' written on it and in the other put a piece of paper with the word 'hate' written on it. Put one pencil in each bag. Mix up the bags so you don't know which is which.

Take a few moments to concentrate. Then open one bag at random and write with the pencil inside. Be sure not to take out the note, so you don't know which one it is. Notice how that pencil feels to write with and what sensations you feel. Decide if that pencil is the one from the 'love' or 'hate' bag.

Check to see if you got it right.

ADD ON

If you didn't get it right the first time, that's absolutely fine. This is definitely an exercise you need to practise and you'll be likely to get clearer energy sensations over time. Be sure not to use the pencils for any other purpose, and when you feel you have done the exercise enough, cleanse the negative energy from the pencil from the 'hate' bag by sending it positive energy or, better still, discard it.

Ritual: Hand on heart

Hear your beat.

WHY?

In every beat your heart is talking to you, but if your life is busy, you won't hear what it has to say. You need calm and silence to hear your heart talking. Your heart really does know what is best for you, so if you are too busy for heartfelt time, perhaps you need to rethink your priorities?

HOW?

Take a few moments to be alone and enjoy peace and quiet.

In those moments, gently place both your hands on your heart. You will feel and hear it beating if you listen closely.

When that happens, close your eyes and focus all your attention just on that beating. Notice the rhythm and speed and how the sound makes you feel. Do you hear your heart whispering to you?

You may not get any messages from your heart at first. You have probably been ignoring it for years, so give it time to adjust to your newfound interest in its pacing. If you keep gently deferring to it, in time it will respond, both with the sound and rhythm of its beats and with calm feelings if something or someone is right for you.

ADD ON

In time you can also turn your meditative focus to opening your heart.

Close your eyes with your hands on your chest and open the eyes of your heart. Feel your heart sending out love to everyone and everything, and as you enter this state of expansiveness, feel the love coming back to you and flowing through you.

Let your heart eyes see beyond the small stuff in your life and connect you to the bigger picture of your life. Sense your interconnection with everyone and everything.

Carry this sense of interconnection[15] between everyone and everything into your everyday life. An open heart dissolves boundaries and is a potent precondition for enlightenment.[16] You can truly sense what quantum physics expounds, which is that we are all a sea of living energy, interconnected energy fields transcending time and space, with each energy vibration, each heartbeat, containing everything in the universe. This is deep inner feeling. It is bliss.

Ritual: Energize your hands

Let your hands do the talking.

WHY?
Your gut and heart are your main sources of information and inspiration, but your hands can also be extremely sensitive to subtle but revealing energy vibrations.

HOW?
Rub the palms of your hands together for thirty seconds and then move them a few inches apart. You may feel they are connected to each other by an invisible warmth that draws them together.

Then slowly move your palms towards each other again. Bring them as close as you can without letting them touch each other.

Now draw them slowly back from each other. Notice what sensations you feel in them. You may feel a tickling sensation or pressure or tension between your palms, or sense a warming up or cooling down.

Repeat this in and out movement.

This is stimulating the energy sensitivity of your hands, so now pick up a random object and tune into it using the awakened sensitivity of your hands. It can be anything – a ring or a pencil or a book. What vibrations are you picking up from that object? The psychic term for object reading is *psychometry*.

ADD ON

Energizing your hands is a great way to tune into your inner psychic's ability to speak to you through your body. Now that you know that your hands can be psychic receptors, pay attention to any signals they may send you when you shake hands with someone or pick up an object.

A fun way to practise this is to find a deck of playing cards and pick out one black card and one red card.

Hold your hand over the black card, close your eyes and notice what impressions you pick up. Do the same with the red card.

Then turn both cards face down, shuffle them and start testing yourself, seeing if your hands can sense the correct colour. You'll be surprised how quickly you improve.

Ritual: First impressions

Be aware of your instant reaction.

WHY?

First impressions can be proved wrong – like Elizabeth and Darcy in *Pride and Prejudice*, often we bring unconscious prejudices and assumptions into our first interactions with others – but more often than not we are spot on with our immediate gut reaction.

HOW?

Whenever you meet someone new, notice what sensations you feel in your stomach and heart. How does that person feel to you? Step into their shoes. Imagine what it would be like being them. What you are tuning into here is their energy vibration.

Now be sure to take a step back and put boundaries back in place. Remind yourself that whatever you pick up from others does not belong to you.

Be sure to make a note of your initial response, and when you get to know that person better, see if your first impressions were correct. If they were, fantastic! If they weren't, this can be helpful because you can try to work out why you were wrong and why you picked up mixed signals. Did that person remind you of someone else or did you assume something?

All your ritual work can offer valuable information. Of course you always want to be spot on with your hunches, but once you understand that getting it wrong can be just as insightful, as it teaches you something valuable about yourself and how your inner psychic speaks to you, it's a win-win situation.

In a nutshell, the more you do this ritual, the better you will get at understanding and relating to the people in your life. You will also not be distracted by what they say or do, because you will listen to your own gut instinct first and sense the truth about their words and actions. And as an added bonus, you will learn a great deal about yourself too.

ADD ON

You can also extend this exercise to the environments and situations you find yourself in. You may feel certain physical sensations, such as warmth or coldness, when you are in a meeting, for example. Or you may notice a body part itching or tightness in your shoulders. Perhaps you enter a room and sense an 'atmosphere', and if you don't feel comfortable in an environment, chances are there's a good reason why. You may dislike how a room looks or smells, of course, but your inner psychic is also picking up on the energy imprints that are there. For instance, a room where loving interactions have taken place will feel different from one which has been the scene of an argument.

You may also want to research the ancient art of *feng shui*, which is all about the careful placement of objects and use of colours to balance energies and create harmony in an environment.

FAQ: 'Why are psychic impressions always so vague?'

Psychic impressions will express themselves in a very gentle way at first for the simple reason that they have got so used to you ignoring them or not noticing them. This can be frustrating when you long for clearer messages, but the way forward is to not force anything but to stay positive and keep on practising. Keeping your eyes closed when you do your exercises can really be useful too, as it helps avoid distractions. And the more you heed its messages, the more your gut will communicate with you.

One fascinating study,[17] which involved exposing participants to emotional images or images that typically triggered positive or negative feelings, such as a cute puppy or a deadly spider, without them actually knowing in advance whether the images were positive or negative, showed that some advance awareness of the unknown content had been expressed through subtle bodily responses. The reason I'm highlighting this study is that the more the participants did this experiment, the better their bodies got at sensing what could not be known, suggesting that your gut instinct can and does improve with practice and reassurance.

Remember it's not your thoughts you are paying attention to, but your feelings, your physical sensations, your very first impressions, usually from your gut and heart, though they can centre on any part of your body. If you are practising these rituals and feel nothing coming through, ask yourself what kind of nothing you are feeling. If you feel good or bad, ask yourself what kind of good or bad you feel. Never accept 'nothing' as the answer. There is always something deeper there for you to find.

Also bear in mind that psychic feeling may not be the optimum or primary way for your inner psychic to reach you. It's entirely possible that it prefers to speak to you through your dreams (see Lesson Four), through your thoughts, or through sounds (Lesson Five).

And as for psychic impressions often feeling vague, this is down to not really understanding the language your inner psychic speaks. It can't speak to you in a logical way because it comes from a place that exists outside logic. It can speak to you through impressions, so your job is to notice them and take them seriously and to then work out what they are trying to tell you or if there is a pattern to them. And the way to do that is exactly the same way you would learn a new language: take notes, uncover meaning and then practise, practise, practise.

BOUNDARY PROTECTION

Boundary protection is an essential psychic/life skill wherever you are on the sensitivity or empathy spectrum. But those who are born with deeply sensitive personality traits[18] must take particular care to protect themselves from the swirl of invisible psychic energies they tune into every day.[19] They are susceptible to confusing the feelings they are empathetically picking up from others with their own.

If, for example, you find yourself feeling inexplicably negative or anxious, you urgently need to go within to calm your mind and unpick what is yours and what is not yours. This is where the vital meditation and contemplative skills you learned in the previous lesson really come into play.

Watch what is happening within you as if you were a witness. Daily meditation will certainly help you detach yourself from your thoughts and feelings. It will also increase your self-awareness and ability to gather the inner strength you need to protect yourself from taking on what is not yours.

DAILY PROTECTION

Here are some powerful daily protection rituals you can perform at any time. All of them can remind you of the importance of setting the intention to protect yourself from absorbing negative energy from people, environments or situations. The power is in that intention and the focus it places on protecting your inner world.

1. Picture yourself in a bubble of protective light. If anything tries to penetrate that bubble, say out loud or in your mind, 'You shall not pass.'
2. Burn sage or light a white candle in your home. Know that this can clear any negative energy that you have brought home with you. You don't have to let the candle burn for long, just a minute or so. Then be sure to snuff it out safely.
3. Put some water into a spritzer and spray yourself and the air around you. Tell yourself this water is protective, sacred and cleansing.
4. Carry a small crystal in your pocket or wear one as jewellery and believe that it will protect you. Selenite is great for cleansing, rose quartz nurtures the heart, amethyst is healing, and ruby and garnet protective. If you prefer, you can simply carry a white feather or a small coin in your pocket. Believing they are protective will bestow them with protective powers.
5. Take a relaxing bath with Epsom salts or with rose or lavender essential oils. If you prefer to shower, imagine you are cleaning away all negative energy that has attached itself to you. Think of your bath or shower time as power cleansing. (Indeed, if you have ever sat in a bath until the water drains out, you'll know this really gives you a clear sense of your body and helps you connect with it.)

6. Throughout the day, every time you drink water, tell yourself that you are drinking in vitality and self-care and absorbing only positive energy. Start carrying a bottle of water around with you, and whenever you feel stressed, sit down and drink it mindfully.

7. Take a few moments alone to close your eyes and slow down your breathing. If you are taking on what isn't yours, your breathing is likely to be shallow and fast. Breathe in slowly through your nose and imagine you are breathing in positivity, and then fully expel all the air from your lungs as you breathe out negativity.

8. Tidy something up in your life. It doesn't matter what. It can be as simple as deleting files you don't use anymore on your home screen or decluttering your bag or purse or pocket. As you declutter, imagine you are removing negative energies from your life.

9. When you feel overwhelmed, pray. You don't need to be religious to pray and you don't need to go down on bended knee either. You can pray with your thoughts. It doesn't matter whom you pray to – a spiritual figure, or an angel, or a tree, or your inner psychic. Whoever it is, simply asking for peace and protection during uncertainty can be effective. Bear in mind that as well as helping protect your energy, prayer can also be healing. Try this: the next time someone dumps things on you that are not yours, send that person silent healing instead of frustration and anger. You'll be surprised how this counterintuitive response can bring you peace, and perhaps them too.

It truly doesn't matter what your psychic protection ritual is. What matters is your belief in it. Feel your own way.[20] You are always the source of your power. Never underestimate your own power. You protect yourself. You set clear boundaries. Every day.

THE WAY TO CONTENTMENT

Everything in this book is steadily leading you towards fully understanding that feeling whole or fulfilled can never be found through other people, work or material stuff. Externals can enhance your experience of life but they can't complete you. For evidence of this, look no further than the lives of the super-rich and famous, who have everything most of us dream of and yet, if they haven't done the inner work and crave constant validation and a sense of identity from the world around them, they hurtle into toxic relationships, anxiety and addiction.

The only way to contentment[21] is to find it in the present moment, independent of whatever is happening in your life. Yes, your inner world can be awash with feelings that have the potential to diminish your joy. But the difference between what goes on in your inner world and what you encounter in the outside world is that you can't control what other people do or what life throws at you, but you can choose your thoughts, feelings and reactions.

The realization that you, and you alone, choose what to allow into your inner world and rule what goes on in there is not just the beginning of all wisdom, it is the moment your inner psychic jumps for joy.

And while on the subject of joy, the next lesson will celebrate your natural-born ability to see clearly with your eyes wide open *and shut*.

LESSON FOUR

What Dreams May Come

Seeing visions is probably what you most strongly associate with being 'psychic'. The specialist term for psychic vision is *clairvoyance*, which means 'clear seeing'.

SEEING CLEARLY

You may have heard stories from people who say they can actually see visions, spirits and angels[1] with their eyes wide open. There is no proof that these visions can't happen, but if one day you join the rare ranks of those who say they can 'see' angels, guides,[2] spirits, fairies or unicorns,[3] please stay humble. Seeing what is invisible doesn't mean you are 'chosen' or that your psychic abilities are superior to those of the vast majority of us who 'see' in our mind's eye. Indeed, internal visions have just as much authority and perhaps even more. Seeing beneath the surface of things is a mighty powerful internal shift that requires the happiness-attracting power of self-belief. To quote the wisdom of Carl Jung, 'Your vision will become clear only when you look inside your heart. Who looks inside, awakens.'

So, what are the *internal* visions that you may not yet have noticed or appreciated because they seem way too 'normal' or familiar?

◐ Your night-time dreams.

◐ The images you 'see' with your mind's eye when you close your eyes.

◐ The symbols, coincidences, shapes and colours you notice in the world around you that feel like signposts guiding you.

◐ The images, pictures or posts, or words in a book or magazine that you feel inexplicably mesmerized by or drawn to.

◐ The visual beauty in the natural world to which you feel a deep sense of connection.

◐ The mental pictures you create when you imagine an outcome.

◐ The light sources you feel drawn to.

◐ The different colours you enjoy experimenting with.

Growing up in a family of psychics where visions were a way of life, not surprisingly I longed to 'see' clearly. But despite my best efforts, I saw nothing with my physical eyes. And not only did I not see visions of angels or spirits, I struggled to create mental images too. It took me decades to comprehend that this 'block' was part of my journey to the contented place I am in today, where I know dramatic visions are not essential for my psychic growth and neither is the ability to create mental imagery. I see clearly in my dreams, memories, intuition, feelings and ideas. I use my inner eyes in ways that work for me.

You'll notice I don't use the word 'visualize' here, and for good reason. Visualization is the ability to picture in your mind's eye what you want to create or see. It's a self-help tool that research[4] has proven is highly successful in helping people reach their goals. It's a great tool for helping to awaken the vision of your inner psychic too, and that's why one of the rituals in this chapter will be devoted to it. But you may be one of those people, like me, for whom it just doesn't come easily, even with understanding, patience and training.

THROUGH A GLASS DARKLY

For many years I felt there was something wrong with me because I just couldn't 'see' consistently in mental pictures. It was hugely demotivating, as many psychic and personal growth courses involve the magical but, for some, elusive power of visualization. That's why it was a tremendous relief when I discovered that scientists now know that some people have a condition called aphantasia,[5] which is an impaired ability to visualize.

If this resonates with you, the good news is that aphantasia doesn't inhibit dream recall – you can still 'see' in your dreams – and it doesn't limit your memory, creativity or imagination either. There are other ways to imagine that you may not have thought of as visualization before. Instead of trying to force mental pictures that won't surface, try describing what you want to see instead. Talk to yourself. Bring the picture to life with your memory, your ability to make associations and your creative ideas/thoughts.

THE EYES HAVE IT

Michael's story:

I woke up around 2 a.m. with a vivid dream on my mind. It felt so real. For a few surreal moments, I wasn't sure if I was still dreaming. In my dream, I was talking to my sister and she told me to buy a new suit because I would need it. I closed my eyes to settle back to sleep and she reappeared again in my mind's eye. We carried on our conversation. She told me to make sure the new suit was blue, not black. I know we spoke about other things, but I couldn't recall what they were. I also didn't know if I was dreaming or awake. It was the strangest thing, but felt incredibly natural and comforting to have a conversation with her again, just like we used to. You see, my sister passed away five years ago. The next day things got stranger. Not only did I get an unexpected bonus at work, but my boss told me to buy a new suit.

Clear seeing is associated with the forehead area in metaphysics. It is believed there is an energy centre or chakra there known as the third eye. Have you ever wondered why the forehead is anointed in some religions?

This matches up with what brain scans reveal. Visual images are interpreted in the frontal lobes, and during rapid eye movement, or REM, stages of sleep, when most dreams occur, there is considerable frontal cortex signalling and very little in the rear lobes. Dreams, of course, are images you see with your mind rather than your eyes. And that is how inner seeing works.

Chances are you have been taught that seeing with your physical eyes is the only real way to see, and because of this, your ability to see with your inner eyes has diminished. But it is still there. You just need to reactivate it and to give it priority over your physical eyes from time to time. Try this little exercise.

Close your eyes. Open them and then close them mindfully. As you close them, notice where your focus naturally goes. It will more often than not be very gently pulled upwards towards your third eye, which is a sign that your body instinctively knows how to activate your inner psychic receptors.

IMAGINATION

Imagination is thinking about or picturing things. It is seeing with your mind's eye rather than with your physical eyes. It isn't the same as clear seeing, more like a receptor for tuning into it, but if you want to see clearly you need to start using your imagination, because it is a trusted bridge to your inner psychic's vision.

When we leave our childhood behind, most of us leave our imagination behind, which is such a loss, as to grow psychically you have to allow yourself to play with infinite possibilities. You have to know how to suspend your disbelief. Of course, being logical and practical matters, and grounds us in the practical world, but there needs to be balance. Without imagination, there would be no progress. Everything starts with a dream or an idea. Everything starts with the magical words 'What if?'

The next time you get a flash or glimpse of imagination, or picture a desired outcome, please, please don't dismiss it. Pay attention. Your inner psychic is using your imagination to create associations and connections that are conducive to receiving psychic wisdom. So, the more you let imagination into your life, the easier it is for your inner psychic to break through.

The following rituals will help liberate your imagination and open your psychic eyes.

Ritual: Open your third eye

See behind your eyes.

WHY?

The energy centre associated with clear seeing is in the middle of your forehead between your eyes. It's called the third eye chakra. Whether it really is an eye or not, it's a beautiful mystical association that you can use to your advantage in this ritual.

HOW?

Close your eyes for a few moments. Notice the upward shift from physical to psychic vision.

Now gently massage in circles the area between your eyes. As you do so, tell yourself that you have a third eye there – your psychic eye – and you are opening it so that you can see both what is seen and unseen.

Then open your physical eyes and notice how different it feels to see with your third eye. Take note of any impressions that reveal themselves to you.

Then shift to seeing with your physical eyes and again notice how different it feels.

During the day, if you ever feel overwhelmed by energies, tell yourself that your third eye is closing or sleeping until you decide to awaken it again.

ADD ON

If you've ever closed your eyes after looking at a candle or light, you'll know you may see the image of that candle or light on your eyelids. Psychic vision is a bit like that. You may want to gently stare at a candle for a few moments – don't look directly into the flame – and after safely snuffing it out, close your eyes. Look at its image on your eyelids until it fades and then add other images using your inner psychic eyes.

Ritual: Get liminal

Watch your own light show.

WHY?

In those twilight stages between waking and sleeping, known as liminal states, you may also become aware of images behind your eyes. When those images come, simply watch and enjoy them, as they can offer a wealth of insight and creativity.

The technical term for this skimming on the surface of sleep state is *hypnagogia*, which actually means 'heading into Hypnos', the Greek god of sleep. (Its twin, less conducive to creativity, skimming on the surface of waking state is *hypnopompia*, meaning 'heading away from Hypnos'.)

The liminal state is not the same as dreaming, where there is often a story or theme, but is simply an egoless state when you can experience all kinds of random images, lights, colours and, on occasion, sounds. It's a prelude to dreaming. However, what you observe and experience at this time can be a revelation. Indeed, hypnagogia is a creativity hack used by the likes of great minds like Thomas Edison. Salvador Dali would famously sit in a chair with a key in his hand, so that when he nodded off and his hand went limp, it would fall to the floor and wake him up. He would then immediately sketch whatever remarkable images he had witnessed in his hypnagogic state.

HOW?

During the day – ideally, mid-afternoon – find somewhere where you can lie down safely and quietly. Set an alarm for ten or fifteen minutes, depending on your schedule.

Lie down and close your eyes. Focus on the sounds going on within you (heartbeat, etc.) and then switch to sounds going on externally and then to sounds further in the distance. If you start to notice images or lights dancing, simply notice them. If nothing appears, observe any feelings or impressions that flow through you.

When the alarm goes off, write down and appreciate any experiences.

ADD ON

If you fall asleep during this exercise, don't get anxious. You clearly need a nap and your alarm will wake you up. There's plenty of research[6] to suggest that a mid-afternoon twenty-minute nap boosts your self-confidence and concentration. And waking from a nap is a big opportunity to recall a dream or two. Short episodes of light sleep increase the likelihood of waking up in REM, the dreaming stage of sleep.

And watching, waiting and noticing what you experience behind your eyes without judgement, resisting the urge to influence or interpret, is an instantly accessible way to not just tap into the hidden depths of liminal, but also reap the proven psychic-empowering benefits of regular meditation.

Ritual: Mind meld

Melt into a picture.

WHY?
Unless you are an artist or involved in highly creative work, chances are you have seriously neglected your imagination. This immersive ritual will remind your rational self that your imagination is a potent force.

HOW?
Search online for a work of art you adore. If you aren't sure what to look for, you can't go wrong with a dreamy, Impressionist Monet or Renoir. Or, perhaps even better, find an illustrated book of fairy tales or a pack of Tarot cards, as both are rich in symbolism.

When you have your image, study it carefully.

If visualization is effortless for you, close your eyes and recreate the image in your mind's eye. Hold it in your mind's eye. Then add in your own colours, ideas and details. Personalize the image. Use all your senses. What are you hearing, feeling, tasting, smelling? Position yourself in the image. Explore. Then leave the picture and allow it to return to its initial form. Open your eyes and look at the image again. Did your mind meld with the picture? Do you have new insights about the image?

If visualization doesn't come naturally to you, study the picture and then look away and describe with your thoughts and your words what you can remember. Pretend to be an art expert describing the image for an interested buyer. Then add in your own creativity[7] and bring the image to life[8] with your words.

Alternatively, you can have a go at drawing the picture and adding in your own details. You aren't trying to create a work of art here. No one is going to see it. Just let your memory and your imagination go wild.

ADD ON

During the day, when you are performing a repetitive task such as walking, tidying up or washing, indulge in a spot of daydreaming. As the routine task keeps your conscious mind busy, visualize or recall uplifting images from your own life or from the movies, or create some right now. Nothing is off-limits. Create and live in a world of your imagination. Please do be aware though that you should not be daydreaming when driving or operating machinery.

Ritual: Watching me, watching you

Perform a daily self-log or personal inventory.

WHY?

An accurate understanding of who you are makes personal improvement and psychic development possible. This ritual is going to ask you to view yourself from a third-party perspective. It will encourage you to detach from your thoughts and feelings so you can identify with the part of you that is separate from all that – your inner psychic.

Viewing yourself this way will also encourage you to make improvements in your life. You will recognize what your needs are, so you can take better care of yourself, and what your strengths and weaknesses are, so changes can be made. Self-awareness opens the door to all personal and psychic growth. Sometimes this can hurt, as you shed old skins, but growth is your purpose. You are here to evolve.

HOW?

Just before sleeping, review your day. Simply rerun it in your mind's eye. Detach from any judgement or thoughts or feelings and see yourself from the perspective of someone who only wants the best for you.

ADD ON

Taking an observational stance and seeing yourself clearly during the day can be extremely helpful whenever you feel overwhelmed. Simply step outside yourself, notice but don't interact with your thoughts or feelings, and connect to the part of you that is separate and can rise above.

And don't go through your waking life on autopilot. Really notice what you are doing. It's incredible how much we often miss with our physical eyes. And the more you see in your waking life, the easier it will be for you to see in other ways. Pay particular attention to coincidences, signs and hidden meanings. Nothing is ever truly straightforward. There are always layers to unpick.

Ritual: Cloud watching

Look up.

WHY?
The natural world is your inner psychic's loving companion. Cloud watching and star gazing are blissful ways to ignite your clear vision.

HOW?
Remember when you were a child and you lay down in the grass and watched the clouds form shapes above you, or tried to create a face or image by connecting the stars? If you don't remember doing this, there's no time like the present. Find somewhere safe to lie down, or sit or stand, and simply gaze at the magical shapes above you. Don't stare intently, just gaze gently, and avoid staring at the sun. See patterns, symbols, signs and pictures forming above you.

ADD ON
And don't stop there. Nature is such a rich source of imagery. Admire a glorious sunrise or sunset. Adore a shimmering lake or the full moon, or wonder at the miracle of a flock of birds and the perfect arrow shape they form.

Remember, too, that people are a part of the natural world. See inner beauty in others and consciously do or say things that help or inspire them. This can be as simple as holding a door open for the person behind you or saying 'thank you' with a warm smile. Notice how your words or actions really can light others up energetically. You'll see that light in their eyes first. It is often said the eyes are the windows to the soul.

Ritual: Your daily chapter

Read some fiction every day.

WHY?

Regularly reading fiction has been shown[9] to help increase creativity and empathy, both of which are psychic super senses. Losing yourself in an alternative reality as you read between the lines and picture the characters and the scenes stimulates your imagination.

HOW?

The ideal time to read fiction is just before bed, because it can help you relax and set you up for a good night's sleep. Any book that offers you an escape into an imaginary world will be just fine. Thirty minutes of bedtime reading will ignite your ability to picture what you want to see or focus your concentration on with your eyes shut.

ADD ON

Poetry speaks the psychic language of symbols and metaphors and associated meanings, so if you feel drawn to it, read it. And don't discount fantasy[10] movies[11] or TV series either, as long as you avoid screens an hour before bed. (*Sandman*, *Inception* and *Lord of the Rings* are my personal dream-boosting screen recommendations.) Reading fiction is preferable, because it requires inner vision to fill in the dots, whereas TV watching is more passive, but films can also sweep you away into an imagined world, which is great practice for creating imaginary worlds of your own.

Visiting an art gallery can also empower your clear seeing. Video gaming too, as long as it's done in moderation and avoided an hour before bedtime. There's a proven[12] connection between gaming and vivid dreaming (I never fail to have big dreams after I play Skyrim).

NOT JUST A DREAM

I toyed with the idea of beginning your inner psychic empowerment programme with your dreams, because dreaming is an immediate and easy-to-access portal to your inner psychic.[13] Dreams remind you of the existence of your mysterious inner world. It's your inner psychic saying 'hi' to you every single night.

We all dream, whatever our belief, culture or age.[14] However, after some reflection I decided to place night visions here in this 'clear seeing' chapter, because the previous lessons have paved the way. I'm hoping all the inner psychic work you've been doing so far is now triggering vivid dreams for you to decode.

A lot of us regard our dream life as separate from our waking life, but investigation[15] reveals that the two influence and comment on one another. Your inner psychic constantly notices things in your waking life that you need to reflect on more, but are ignoring. So, you encounter those in your dreams.[16]

Increasingly, psychologists and scientists[17] are regarding dreams not as random brain activity, but as some kind of mood-regulating system or continuation of reality that can help you work through any problems, fears and challenges you may have in waking life. Experts believe dreams can also assist in problem-solving, learning, memory storage, creativity and changing behaviour.[18]

As you are already dreaming (everyone is), you are already clear seeing. You've likely been dismissing your dreams as inconsequential.[19] Perhaps at school or at some point you were told that dreams were simply your brain's way of decluttering or offloading at night. But nothing could be further from the truth. Let's not waste any more precious dream time and dive head first into your night visions.

WHILE YOU ARE SLEEPING

You've already discovered how important meditation is for awakening your psychic potential. The Dalai Lama once said the best meditation was to sleep,[20] and when you sleep, of course you dream, which is to say your unconscious – the place where there is just infinite possibility and no sense of logic, time or space – sends you clear visions.

The 'Sleep on it' advice is not only age old, it is spot on. Every time you fall asleep, you have an incredible opportunity to reflect on situations in your waking life from a different perspective – the perspective of your inner psychic. Dreams are the most common but neglected way for your inner psychic to present information to you through clear seeing.

Every time you wake up with dreams on your mind, it truly is a cause for gratitude and celebration. Your inner psychic has something to share with you, and even if you aren't able to decipher the meaning of its images, they are a powerful reminder that there is so much more to you than meets the eye. Every night you go to a place outside time and space.

The majority of modern sleep researchers[21] now suggest that in the symbolic language of the unconscious, dreams bring important things for our personal growth to the surface, and regular dream recall is a sign of increased mental, emotional and psychological well-being.

Scientists don't really know for sure why we dream or sleep, but they do know that if deprived of REM sleep, which, as you will remember, is the stage of sleep when most dreams happen, we suffer anxiety and swifter mortality. Perhaps, then, the reason we sleep might just be to dream?

DREAM POWER

'A single dream is more powerful than a thousand realities.'

J. R. R. Tolkien

Think of your dreams as your internal therapist. They offer brain-storming insights, outside-the-box perspectives, catharsis and deep insight into your waking life. They are a bit like a mirror. If you don't like your dreams, making changes in your waking life can change them for the better.

Dreams are potent tools for self-awareness, as they symbolically highlight your hopes and fears so you can work through issues in your waking life and discover hidden creativity. Indeed, an effective creativity hack is to simply write down or describe one of your dreams. In no time at all you will find that this sweeps away any writer's block.

Even nightmares have a cathartic effect, because when you wake up, you know you have faced your fears and now can understand them better and hopefully move on from them. Think of night-mares as a transformative gift – your dreaming mind's attempt to heal you, rather like a fever is a sign of your body healing.

NIGHT VISION

Although the majority of your dreams will be symbolic, a small percentage – around 1 per cent or less – will have a very different feel to them. Whereas symbolic dreams tend to be like fragments in a music video, some dreams feel more realistic and have a clear beginning, middle and end.

I'm absolutely convinced, given the stories I am sent and my own experience and research on precognition,[22] that dreams can showcase psychic elements.[23] I call such dreams *night visions*, and these visions include shared dreams (someone you know has the same dream as you at the same time), telepathic dreams (you dream about something that you can't possibly know and it turns out to be true), precognitive dreams (you glimpse a potential future), dreams of departed loved ones, and lucid dreams[24] (you know you are dreaming when you are dreaming and can potentially influence that dream and role play). Lucid dreaming is the Holy Grail of dreaming and a massive confidence boost, but it does require diligent patience and practice.[25] (If you want to explore this further, I cover it fully in my Harper Thorsons book *How to Catch a Dream*.)

FUTURE VISION

Have you ever had a dream and a few days later elements of that dream have played out? Dr Stanley Krippner,[26] who is well known for his research into precognitive dreams, had a dream in which he saw a hearse pull up to his childhood home. It took away his father, his next-door neighbour and the father of a grade-school class-mate. His father and his next-door neighbour died within months of his dream, and the grade-school classmate's father died within a year.

Since the future can be sensed when you are awake, it makes sense that it can also happen when you are asleep and dreaming.[27] Indeed, it's more likely to, because linear time only exists in your conscious state, but in your unconscious, all time – past, present and future – is happening at the same time.

In the dream state, you can encounter all your past and future selves, and this extended sense of yourself existing over time and space is a transcendent experience. Although the idea of having a 'long self'[28] over time, an idea from the Native American Iroquois tribe, sounds mind-blowing, it is actually remarkably comforting. Thinking of yourself as all versions of yourself, through time and space, is a deeply healing inner psychic shift. You can travel in your mind back to your past and be there for yourself during times of trauma, and may even start to think of your future self watching over you right now like a guardian angel. If you think this sounds way out there, a gentle reminder that science points towards the universe being evolutionary and infinite, so in an evolutionary universe surely the laws of time and space themselves can also evolve? And in an infinite universe, surely it is not such a stretch to think about your consciousness as infinite, too?

Computer scientist, space-mission designer and origin-of-life researcher Dr Bruce Damer[29] put forward the revolutionary theory that life on Earth began in fluctuating volcanic pools on land, which created 'protocells'. From an early age, Damer felt he was in communication with his future and that he was in a relationship with some kind of bigger guiding force. In his teens, he had a vision. In this vision his mind travelled back thousands of years and returned with these protocells and they talked to him.

Damer believes this vision was sent to him by his future self. It prompted him to make an 'only positive visions' contract with his future selves, so that they all agreed not to send negative thoughts back to the prior selves, because they did their best at the time. Once Damer signed this contract, he experienced a rush and a feeling that all the doors to his future were pulling him.

Damer's case illustrates how powerful it can be to take seriously visions and dreams of your potential future. You start to include future and past versions of yourself as part of your definition of yourself. This doesn't mean you know what the future will bring, as you always have free will. The future is not fixed. It is created by your present. But thinking of all your selves across space and time in this expansive way is another important inner shift.

MESSAGES

As compelling as they are, don't fall into the trap of thinking that psychic dreams are of more value than symbolic ones. Symbolic dreams increase your self-awareness, and self-awareness is vital for your psychic empowerment. Every single dream you have is a special message from your inner psychic. I also believe that every dream has a precognitive element, offering insight about a potential future.

And if you are wondering why your precognitive dreams can sometimes focus on what appears trivial – for example, you dream about a purple scarf and the next day on a train find yourself sitting beside someone wearing that purple scarf but have no connection to that person – remember that nothing is ever trivial. Your dreaming mind is highlighting the colour purple and a scarf for a reason. Brainstorm. Think about the time you noticed the purple scarf in real life. What were you thinking? Where were you going? That moment in time has a message for you.

THE PREMONITION CODE

In 2017 I fully explored the science and evidence for precognitive dreaming in *The Premonition Code*, a book I co-authored with cognitive neuroscientist Dr Julia Mossbridge,[30] who also co-authored, with psychology professor Imants Barušs, *Transcendent Mind*, published by the American Psychological Association, their first book to suggest that your mind or consciousness can exist separately from your brain and body.

Precognitive dreams that are completely accurate are rare, but they can happen. Many people reported dreams of planes and towers collapsing before 9/11 and others, myself included, had mask-themed dreams before the pandemic hit in late 2019.

Far more likely, though, are dreams that offer glimpses of potential futures which will occur if you don't make changes in your waking life. These dreams are just as incredible, as they give you an opportunity to preview potential outcomes, and if you don't like the future you glimpsed in your dreams, you can make changes in your present.

These potential future dreams show that the future is not fixed and you always have the potential to change it by the actions you take and the feelings and beliefs you have in the present – the power of now. To offer a metaphor, if you hold a ball in your hand and decide to drop it, its future is to hit the ground. But what if after you drop it you change your mind and decide to catch it? Its future changes!

Your inner psychic is eternally in love with the power and potential of your now, both when you are awake and when you are dreaming.

Now that your attention has been drawn to your remarkable night vision, let *your* dream games begin.

Ritual: The album

Track your dreams.

WHY?

A way to connect to your inner vision that has been proven[31] to be effective is to keep a dedicated dream journal.

Think of it in the same way as photos stored on your phone – snapshots which covey the essence of what you are experiencing. You collate those images because they mean something to you. Your dream journal is your dream album.

HOW?

Writing down any dream memories should take you no more than a few minutes on waking from a sleep or nap. But you do need to commit to keeping this record every waking time from now on.

Every night before you go to bed, be sure to place a blank piece of paper or a journal to write in and a pen you enjoy writing with beside your bed. Tell yourself that you are going to have wonderful dream recall in the morning. If you know it will be dark when you wake, place a night light or torch there too. Bless your dream journal by placing your hand on it before you go to sleep, if that speaks to you.

When you wake up in the morning – hopefully naturally rather than with an alarm, because alarms create psychic-diminishing stress and tear you away from your dreams too abruptly – keep still and don't blink. Any movement or sudden noise signals to your conscious, rational mind that it is time to take over, and your unconscious mind – where your dreams come from – can't compete.

So, keep still for those first few moments and see if any images surface. Check in with your body to see if any dream memories lie there.

As soon as images, feelings or stories come through, sit up and write them down *immediately*. Don't wait until you have been to the bathroom or got dressed, etc., as any movement, even blinking, pushes you further into conscious reality and away from dream recall.

Write your dream memories down in the present tense, as this helps keep the dream alive and fresh. Forget about correct grammar or good handwriting. Focus on the general themes and feelings, rather than every single detail. Write down anything that comes to mind. Any image, colour, symbol, impression, thing, place, sound, etc., could matter. If the details are vague, hone in on the feeling you woke up with, as that will be related to your dream in some way.

Don't try to make the dream memories coherent or force them to make sense at this stage.

Don't worry if nothing comes through. It's normal not to have dream recall every morning, especially if your waking life is so busy there is no space for your dreams to break through. Simply ask your dreaming mind to talk to you the next time you dream or when you are ready.

When you have finished, make a note of the time and date and moon phase (*see below*).

Leave the interpretation for now and get on with your day. You need some distance so you can be more objective when you do interpret your dream.

Carrying a notepad around during the day may be helpful, as dream memories may suddenly pop into your mind. They are most likely to do this when something you do in the day triggers a memory, or when you are doing something routine, such as showering, walking or driving. When your conscious mind is busy with the activity, it temporarily suspends its dominance, allowing your unconscious mind – your inner psychic – to surface.

ADD ON

Drawing your dream can be an effective way of recalling it. And another great way to trigger dream recall is to tell a loved one or close friend your dream. The act of describing it will bring dream images to the surface, but be sure to share your dreams only with people you trust, as they are an intimate glimpse of your soul.

You may want to keep a diary of your waking life and dream life together.[32] Ideally, you should do this with one side of the page for your waking life and the other for your dream life. In the evening before bed, write down your waking experiences, and then in the morning when you wake up, write down your dreams. Recording your dreams alongside your waking experiences is a great way to see how your dreams are commenting like a poetic voice-over on your waking life and how your waking life is influencing your dream life.

You will also come to understand that dreams are better understood in combination with other dreams. Simply focusing on one dream isn't enough. You need to see your dreams as a series of reflections. Dreams are like a long-running TV series. You need to see patterns developing over time. For this reason, dream work is best done in *hindsight*.

Ritual: Show and tell yourself

Set your dream intentions.

WHY?
Your mind believes what you tell it repeatedly, so if you keep telling yourself you don't remember your dreams, you won't, but repeating positive statements,[33] especially when you are most receptive, just before falling asleep, can really boost dream recall. Affirmations, remember, work by interrupting and overriding negative beliefs that are creating mental blocks and replacing them with positive ones – in this case dream-recalling ones.

HOW?
Before you go to sleep at night, look at your pillow as if it were a face or a mirror and repeat out loud or in your mind:

Tonight my dreams will show themselves to me and in the morning when I wake up I will have clear dream recall.

Put your belief into this affirmation. And say or think it with a sense of expectation, trust and joy. Know that what you tell yourself before sleeping will be stored in your unconscious, where it will influence your dreams. So, make your intention-to-dream statement every single night and then sleep on it.

If you feel faintly ridiculous talking to yourself, that's good. Have a good laugh at yourself. Taking yourself less seriously works wonders when it comes to empowering your inner psychic through dream work. After all, in the madcap world of your dreams, the only thing you can be certain of is the craziness that you will encounter there.

ADD ON

Once your dream recall and dream tracking are well established and the relationship between you and your dreaming mind is strong, take things further. Before you go to sleep, ask your dreaming mind to offer you insights into issues in your waking life that you want help with. Bear in mind your dreaming mind won't give you definitive answers, as answers often shut down further exploration, but it will help you brainstorm and send you perspectives you haven't considered before. Every dream has the same goal: to help you learn more about yourself and evolve.

You may also ask your dreaming mind to send you a dream about something you want to happen so you can experience how it feels. The more you feel the energy of what you want, the more likely you are to attract that energy into your life. Indeed, dreaming about something that you long for in your waking life, for example a pay rise, is a sign that your inner psychic is preparing the way. You are closer than ever to achieving your goals because your belief in your own ability is a magnet attracting it.

Ritual: Dreaming around the moon

Align your dream work with the phases of the moon.

WHY?

There is a clear link between the moon and dreams, as both come out at night. In many traditions, there is also a clear link between the moon and the unconscious, or inner world.

In ancient times people lived in tune with nature and the phases of the moon in order to have an understanding of time and when to harvest, rest, celebrate and plant.[34] The moon exerts a gravitational pull on the tides, stabilizes the Earth and impacts the seasons,[35] so ancient thinking may not be primitive thinking. And as a large portion of your body is water, perhaps the moon can exert a gravitational pull on you too and bring all that is unconscious to the surface in your intuition by day and your dreams by night.

Aligning your dream work with the energy of the phases of the moon is a powerful way to boost your night vision.

HOW?

Modern life has disrupted our ancient bonds to the moon, but it is simple to get back in tune with it. There are many moon phases, but for dream work you only need to focus on the four main phases of the twenty-eight/twenty-nine-day lunar cycle or month.

The new or crescent moon

The new or crescent moon is when the moon is barely visible in the sky. The qualities associated with new moon energies are beginnings and the intention-setting needed to set everything in motion.

During this phase, focus on underlining the importance of what you do first thing in the morning and last thing at night. On waking, be sure to write down your dreams, and before sleep, set the clear intention to dream.

The waxing moon

The waxing moon is when the moon becomes more and more visible in the sky. The qualities associated with waxing moon energies are action, discipline and self-belief.

During the waxing phase, continue to pay attention to and record your dreams but shine the nightlight on your sleep hygiene too. Sounds obvious, but if you don't get a good night's sleep, you are going to struggle with dream recall. So, ensure your bedroom is a place of comfort and peace. And don't forget the connection between your waking and dream life. During the day, surprise and inspire your waking mind. Give your inner psychic plenty to reflect on in your dreams.

The full moon

The full moon occurs for a couple of days around day fifteen of the lunar month and this is when it is entirely revealed and lights up the night sky. The qualities associated with full moon energies are self-awareness, fulfilment and celebration.

The full moon is the ideal time to start decoding your dreams in earnest. If you've been recording them during the previous moon phases, you'll have plenty of material to work with and decode in hindsight. Remember, as you interpret, that your dreams speak to you in the language of symbols, and the great majority of them are all about you and your state of mind.

The waning phase
The waning phase is when the moon gradually grows less visible in the sky until the end of the lunar month, when it can't be seen at all. This is the dark moon. The qualities associated with the waning and dark moon are reflection, healing, letting go and acceptance.

The waning and dark moon are perfect times to reflect on the meaning of your dreams and to learn your own personal symbolic language. If you experience nightmares, see them as an opportunity to face and understand your shadow[36] side in a safe way. There is negative potential within us all. What matters is the positive choices we make. Always seek the positive in your dreams. For example, if you dream of death, remind yourself that death is a symbol of endings, but with every ending comes the excitement of a new beginning. And if nightmares are causing distress, a healing technique is to rewrite them.

This moon phase is also the ideal time to ask questions of your dreams.

Also bear in mind that dreaming about the kind of life you want to live can be a powerful manifesting technique. Your brain doesn't know the difference between dreaming and waking, so if you experience something in a dream, your brain knows it's possible. And with self-belief and positive expectation, you raise your psychic vibration and your chances of attracting the success you dream of skyrocket.

In 1999, film-maker Timothy Schultz[37] had a dream that he would win the lottery and a few months later he did – to the tune of $10 million. He was just twenty-one at the time and one of the youngest winners of the Powerball lottery in the US. And contrary to what you may think, dreaming of winning the lottery is actually rare – it's never been in the top 100 commonly reported dreams chart. Yes, there is a dreams chart!

ADD ON

A spot of moon bathing before you go to sleep may help you connect to your nocturnal intuition. Gaze gently at the moon from a window or go outside and stand in the moonlight for a few minutes. If you can't see the moon because it is the dark of the moon, or a cloudy night, find a picture of it online or see it in your mind's eye. Placing a moonstone or amethyst or rose quartz or other crystal associated with dreaming beside your bed may also boost vivid dreaming.

FAQ: 'I rarely recall my dreams, and if I do, they don't make sense. How can I improve my dream recall and also understand my dreams better?'

Brain scans show that we dream at least five or six times every night, so there is no question you are dreaming. The issue is recalling your dreams. But dream recall is something everyone can learn to do with a few simple changes in routine.

To increase your chances, be sure to put a pen and notebook beside your bed as a visual reminder that you are going to have dreams that you will record on waking. Then, just before you drift off to sleep, tell yourself that you are going to dream and that it will be fun.

When you wake up, remember to keep still with your eyes closed for a few minutes rather than immediately jumping out of bed.

Sometimes recalling a dream you had in the past can help trigger a connection to your dreaming mind, so you could try that if you don't recall anything immediately.

If you wake up and can't remember anything at all, don't worry. Just write down in your notebook that you can't recall your dream today but perhaps you will tomorrow. Simply writing something in your dream notebook shows your dreaming self that you are serious about your dream work.

Taking your dreams seriously, thinking more about them during the day and writing daily in your dream journal will all increase your chances of dream recall. Your dreaming mind is craving your attention, but if you have been ignoring or dismissing it for years, it is going to take a while to trust you again. Also, if you are going through stress in your waking life, dream recall is often a casualty, so daily meditation to connect to a calm inner place is highly recommended. Keep repeating your dreamwork rituals and trust that behind the scenes your dreams truly are working on your behalf. Believe in and feel grateful for their beauty, both the ones you remember and the ones you don't.

There are a few practical things you can do to aid dream recall too, such as getting enough vitamin B in your diet, in particular B6 which is found in foods such as bananas, carrots, green leafy vegetables and sunflower seeds, and establishing good sleep hygiene, nourishing your dreaming mind with fantasy novels, books and games, and having a curious, open-minded attitude. Your dreaming mind takes inspiration from your waking life, so do what you can during the day to inspire magical dreams.

And when those dream memories do start flowing through, understand them better with these dream-decoding fundamentals.

Dream language

Your dreaming mind talks to you like a poet or an artist, using symbols and metaphors. Your job is to decode these. In ancient times people had an instinctive understanding of symbols, but in modern times we have lost that ability and need to relearn it.

Here's a great tip: go back in your mind to your school days,[38] when you were asked to interpret a poem by exploring its metaphors, symbolism, pathetic fallacies, figurative language, foreshadowing, puns, alliteration, assonance, and so on. This is the artistic and visionary language of your dreams. Pick them apart in the same way.

Rule out any literal explanation first. For example, if you dream of your teeth falling out, do you need to visit the dentist? If, however, a dream bears absolutely no relation to the present moment – your dreams are about your present even if they use symbols from your past to express that – it's time to reflect on its symbolic meaning and what insights into your life it is revealing and what opportunities for growth it is presenting.

A hall of mirrors

The great majority of your dreams will be symbolic visions of your inner world. They're all about *you*.[39] Every symbol and scenario typically represents something about you and your waking life. If other people appear in a dream, do brainstorm first to see if the dream is telling you something symbolically about them. But more often than not, you're not actually dreaming about them but a part of yourself that they represent and that you have been neglecting or need to understand better or integrate into your life.

Dreaming really is like stepping into a hall of fairground mirrors. Ask yourself what aspect of yourself all the features of your dream represent. What do you need to face, acknowledge, express, heal or integrate?

A great place to start with dream decoding is to ask, 'What does this dream mean to me?' or 'What does this symbol mean to me?' You can consult dream dictionaries online, or my HarperCollins *Dream Dictionary A to Z* (originally published as *The Element Encyclopedia of 20,000 Dreams*) as a way to kick-start your symbolic thinking, but bear in mind dream dictionaries provide the universal meanings of common dream symbols and they may not be applicable to you.

Personal association is always the first and last lesson. For example, if you love dogs (a symbol of unconditional love and loyalty), when a dog appears in a dream it will have that meaning for you, but it will have a very different meaning for someone who fears them. If *you* think your dream has a certain meaning, you're right.

Locations often hold powerful clues. For example, if you are back at school, what is the lesson?

Any kind of motion or mode of transport suggests the direction you are heading in. Water is emotion. Colours have messages too.

And pay attention to your role in the dream. Are you in the thick of it or an observer? If you don't like your role, know that you can change it.

Dreams also love to pun, so bear that in mind, and also bear in mind the element of surprise – your dreams will often tell you what you don't already know!

When a dream symbol surfaces, use the free association technique where you write down the first thing that comes to mind. Then brainstorm. What is your dream telling you about yourself?

You'll know when you've hit on the right interpretation because you'll get an 'Aha!' moment of clarity. The right interpretation will also feel energizing and positive rather than draining. If a dream interpretation diminishes or disappoints you in any way, it's not the right interpretation. The correct meaning will always energize and uplift you because your dreaming mind is expansive.

Get more info

If insight doesn't come from brainstorming a dream, simply ask your dreaming mind to be more specific and give it several nights and dreams to speak to you more clearly. Dreams are like a long-running TV series – they comment on and continue each other – so don't get hung up on interpreting one dream in isolation.

Recurring dreams

This is a form of tough love. If you experience recurring dreams, this is because you haven't understood the message of that dream in your waking life, so your dreaming mind keeps repeating the point. As soon as you do understand the meaning, the recurring dream will stop.

Don't stress

If after all this, you still don't understand a specific dream, please don't stress. Some dreams aren't meant to be understood, but to ignite your curiosity and sense of infinite possibility and mystery. Simply feel grateful for any dreams that reveal themselves to you – they are evidence that your inner psychic is waking up.

Get all over yourself

Every single time you decode your dreams you are empowering your inner psychic, because you are understanding yourself better from the inside out. Research from psychologist Daniel Goldman[40] suggests that a deep understanding of yourself is crucial for success. And the more self-aware you are, the more psychic you will become. Think of it this way: you can't evolve if you don't know what your challenges and strengths are, and every single dream you have encourages you to acknowledge both your best and worst qualities.

And a great side-effect of dream work is that you will also become less dependent on others 'getting' you. You won't need their validation. Too many of us waste our energy and potential trying to get others to 'get' us. This is so important it deserves capitals: YOU NEED TO GET YOURSELF FIRST. Then you'll feel less and less need to convince others of your worth.

Dream work[41] is your loyal and trusty companion on the royal road to self-awareness and from there to the magic of self-belief.

Never enough

When you love both your day and night-time dreams, you start to fall in love with yourself, and that is when all true magic begins. It is also when you see more clearly.

But although clear seeing is a stunningly immediate and accessible way to meet your inner psychic, it is not the only way. Perhaps the most remarkable thing about your inner psychic is that once it captures your attention, it will find more and more enterprising ways to show itself to you.

Let's count more of these loving ways in the next chapter. Like your psychic vision, they are so eager to be noticed and have so much to tell you ...

LESSON FIVE
Psychic Notes

'We are such stuff as dreams are made on,' and as we begin this next lesson, just allow these immortal words of Shakespeare to linger on your mind and settle in your heart and soul.

In the previous lesson you learned that your dreaming and waking mind aren't separate and your inner psychic offers insights and comments on your waking life in the language of symbols in your dreams. Dream work increases your self-awareness. But you can create an even greater transformational shift by bringing your newfound dream-decoding skills into your waking life.

Start questioning, reflecting on and living your life as if it were a dream to decode. Bring that playful, expansive, symbolic, creative sense of infinite possibility into your waking life. Bring that understanding that you are not what you *do* or what you *have* or even what you *think*, you are what is *going on within you*. Look for the deeper or true meaning behind everyone and everything. See connections, associations. Notice coincidences. Signs. Experiment. Live lucidly. Live deep.

Just like a dream, nothing in your waking life is ever what it seems. Search beneath the surface. Embrace the wisdom of opposites. Life, again like a dream, can often be incomprehensible and messy, but although night is opposite to day, they need each other to exist. If you can't understand something or find the deeper meaning in it, let it go and trust that it is happening for a reason and when the time is right more and more revelations will come.

MORE, MORE, MORE ...

Dream work may very well become your way to empower your inner psychic when your eyes are closed *and* open, or perhaps trusting your gut or the way your body whispers to you resonates more. Although the themes of the previous two chapters – clear feeling and clear seeing – are potent psychic senses, there are other senses which may actually be your preferred medium. But even if they aren't, it is important that you know they are psychic potentials already within you.

In this lesson, techniques to activate your clear-knowing, clear-hearing and aura-sensing abilities will be explored, as well as a brief insight into mind–body healing. By the end you will have all the illumination you need to recognize and start using the full spectrum of your innate psychic senses.

CLEAR KNOWING

Clear knowing (claircognizance) is unexpectedly and instantly knowing what is the best thing to do or say or what should or will happen. There's no physical sensation or mental picture or dream or anything else to accompany it. It's just a knowing thought.

Pam's story:

My husband and I had friends who were trying for a baby. One weekend in May they came for a short visit and shared that they had recently had a miscarriage. We commiserated with them. When they left our home, we looked out of the window and as they went down the steps of the porch, quietly and without warning I announced to my husband, 'She will be pregnant again in August and will have a little boy.' And in August she was pregnant and went on to have a healthy baby boy.

Clear knowing may also be about the past. Incomprehensible things that happened days, months or years ago may suddenly make sense. It is often confused with 'genius' or 'cleverness' or 'expertise', but it is a natural psychic sense. It's also the fastest and can happen quite literally in the blink of an eye, so that sometimes you barely notice it at the time. In metaphysics it is often associated with the energy centre or chakra located at the crown of the head.

To help you get a better sense of it, try this exercise:

Close your eyes, consciously shifting your line of vision and awareness upwards to the top of your head (without moving your head upwards), and notice what thoughts and sensations you experience. It can help to think of a shaft of light or a cord at the top of your head pulling all your awareness up. Psychic knowing is looking and feeling upwards. It's elevating your awareness and your thinking to a higher level.

Another way to get an understanding of clear knowing, you can use hindsight. Cast your mind back for a moment. Have you ever had the experience of just knowing something was going to happen and it did? Or just knowing what someone would say next and then they did? This isn't quite the same as precognition or future sensing, as you don't get a glimpse or feeling of a potential future; you just inexplicably know exactly what's going to happen next.

People who have highly developed psychic knowing typically seem to know what is current or what the key issues are or what is the best thing to say or do next. They are the fast-moving disruptors who bring about much-needed innovation. They have a reputation for being lucky and fearless and are often the restless investors and entrepreneurs, authors, artists, designers and movie directors who create trends and bring the future into the present. They are ahead of their time.

Clear knowing tends to happen spontaneously and doesn't really respond well to any attempts to force it artificially, but you can encourage it with the following rituals.

Ritual: Insight timer

Record your clear knowing.

WHY?
The most common reason you don't tap into the potential of clear knowing is that it is so instant, fleeting and immediate that you don't have time to notice it when it strikes, or if you do notice, you dismiss it as trivial or irrational, allowing secondary thoughts to distract you.

HOW?
Before a meeting, or whenever you meet someone new or visit a place you haven't been before or find yourself in an unexpected situation, be sure to shift your thinking and awareness upwards and notice your first *thoughts*, however nonsensical. Don't even give yourself a chance to blink, as even blinking redirects your thoughts. Make a note of them. This may not always be easy to do, as you can't shake someone's hand and then pull out your notebook and start

writing, but be sure to make at least a mental note. Then when you get a chance, make a written or typed record of those very first insights, even if the meeting or experience as it played out apparently proved the opposite. Only time will tell if your first insight was right. Hindsight is the greatest teacher when it comes to clear knowing.

And if those thoughts weren't right, you can still learn from them. What assumptions or prejudices were you projecting onto the situation? Sometimes an insight can teach you more about yourself than someone or something else, and that's great news, as psychic empowerment is an ongoing process of self-knowledge.

ADD ON
Have fun testing your clear knowing. When a text comes in, notice your first thought about who it might be from and then see if it is correct. Before you switch on the TV or radio or open your email, or when the doorbell rings, do the same. What do you think will be on? Who has emailed you? Who is at the door?

Ritual: Remote viewing

View something remote.

WHY?
'Remote viewing' is a term used to describe the alleged ability to get a sense of a location without ever having visited it before. It is an advanced form of clear knowing.

HOW?

Pick a place you have never visited or seen before but which one day you can actually visit. (This may be a challenge, as so much information is available online these days. And this ready availability of information online is one of the reasons our inner psychic has got used to sleeping.) I recommend a restaurant that isn't part of a chain, or a friend's house, or a colleague's office.

Then, with just the location in mind, and with no substantial knowledge of any other details, raise your awareness to the top of your head and notice what insight or thought comes through.

When you get a chance to visit that location, see how accurate your sense of the place was. Don't beat yourself up if you missed the mark. Failed experiments are just as informative as successful ones. They're all data you can use to inform and ultimately empower your inner knowing.

CLEAR HEARING

Clear hearing (clairaudience) is receiving guidance, inspiration and comfort from your inner psychic through sound – through hearing words, discussions, noises and music internally and, on rare occasions, externally. In metaphysics it is associated with the energy centres just a few inches above your ears. Generally, the sound is gentle, but sometimes it can become urgent and forceful and simply grabs your attention. I have personal experience of this.

My story:

In my early thirties I had a dream of my departed mother, who told me to take the right path. This was something she used to tell me when she was alive, meaning 'Take the positive path,' so I thought nothing of it. The next day when I was wide awake and driving my car to a busy junction, I heard the same dream voice inside my head calmly telling me to turn right when I needed to be heading left to get to where I wanted to be. My split-second decision to obey without question that inexplicable inner voice meant I avoided a crash that killed three people, one of whom could have been me.

Hearing voices is often considered to be the first sign of madness. I'm a little nervous including that, but, although my family may disagree at times, I'm not mad! And clear hearing can't be confused with psychiatric conditions, because in all cases psychic sounds are positive, empowering and uplifting. If the voices you hear are negative, draining and controlling, seek advice from your doctor or a counsellor. This isn't your inner psychic talking to you.

Clear hearing can be easy to confuse with self-talk or thinking out loud, but there is a difference. Clear hearing will be calm, concise, consistent and clear. Self-talk, on the other hand, tends to ramble and contradict itself. It is like listening to the sound of your voice and will also feel draining, whereas clear hearing will always be gentle and positive and the voice will be more generic.

A sure-fire sign you are tuning into your clear hearing is that you become more assertive in your everyday life. You follow the facts, create plans that work and your actions speak louder than your words.

Ritual: Ask yourself

Fine-tune your inner ears.

WHY?
Knowing how to switch from hearing with your physical ears to hearing your inner psychic will help you identify clear hearing.

HOW?
Close your eyes and listen carefully to all the sounds going on around you in the external world. Then gently massage the sides of your head above your ears for a few moments. Consciously shift your awareness to the sides of your head.

Listen keenly to what is going on within you. Your breath and heart rate are a good place to start. Then listen to what sounds or words you can hear on the inside. If there is silence, celebrate that. Sometimes silence can say much more than words.

After a few moments, switch back to hearing externally before focusing internally again.

Keep doing this switching in and out until you get a clear sense of the difference between external and internal hearing.

Then, when you are tuned inwards, ask your inner psychic to send you a word or phrase that you need to know right now.

Write down whatever comes through.

The more you practise this inner hearing technique, the easier it will be for you to become your own counsellor whenever you need answers or inspiration. It's incredibly liberating tuning into the wisdom of your own inner voice.

ADD ON
In your daily life, extend your listening skills as often as you can. Consciously decide to talk less and listen more to your inner wisdom while others do the talking. You'll be amazed how much more you learn about them and about yourself.

Listening to music you love every day can also fine-tune your inner hearing. In my *White Shores* podcast I make a conscious effort to include music[1] and interview musicians as often as I can. There's method in my madness, as the sound of music you love can speak directly to your soul. It can also incubate sweet dreams.[2]

Research[3] shows music[4] can induce calm because it helps build a healing bridge between the logical part of your brain (as you try to make sense of musical patterns) and the creative part of your brain (which carries you to unseen places as you listen). Studies also suggest that if listening to music gives you goosebumps,[5] your brain is predisposed to greater empathy and sensitivity, suggesting that the more music you listen to, the better your psychic growth.

Here is a sample of just some of the music that never fails to give me goosebumps, but be sure to curate your own psychic hit list. As you can see, I adore film and classical music, but there is no musical genre that you can't include. Here's my list:

- Rachmaninov, Piano concerto number 2
- Mozart, Requiem
- Hans Zimmer, *Pirates of the Caribbean* theme song
- James Horner, *Titanic* score
- Elgar, Cello concerto

☾ Beethoven, 'Moonlight' sonata
☾ Howard Shore, *Lord of the Rings* score
☾ 'Greensleeves'
☾ Enya and Kate Bush songs

I'd love to hear what your list is, so feel free to get in touch and send it to me.

As we get older, many of us stop listening to music, and that is such a loss for our clear hearing. Other things we stop doing so much are skipping, singing and dancing. But psychic empowerment is celebration. It doesn't matter if you are a good dancer or singer. Stop taking yourself so seriously!

If you don't want to dance or sing, it can suggest you don't want to laugh, love or live life to the full. Put this book down and listen to a song or piece of music right now that makes you want to dream[6] or sing along or move, even if that is just tapping your fingers to the music. And the next time you are walking and you feel safe to do so, break into a skip. See how it feels!

SACRED SOUNDS

You may want to tune into the sound world available for you online, ranging from ambient sounds and natural sounds on YouTube to brainwave entrainment with binaural beats.[7] The majority of these tracks are entirely free ways for you to use the power of sound-waves to awaken your clear hearing. Enjoy.

And don't forget the most glorious music that can be found in nature. If you are an early riser, listen to the dawn chorus, or seek out birdsong where you can in parks or green places. If you can't do that, listening to an audio of birdsong can be highly therapeutic. Or seek out a stream, river, lake, sea or ocean and see if the sound of water speaks to you through the thoughts and feelings it inspires within you. There is a whole mysterious blue world[8] beneath the surface of water, just as there is a whole mysterious world within you.

Ritual: Time machine

Talk to yourself over time.

WHY?

Promising research[9] pioneered by TILT (The Institute of Love and Time, *see page 239*) suggests that lovingly recording voice messages to internal representations of your past and future selves increases overall well-being. As an added bonus, it can also give you an expansive sense of yourself existing outside space and time.

HOW?

Every day on your phone, record a loving and empowering voice message for your future self or the person you are going to be tomorrow. If you find this hard, speak to yourself in the same way you would speak to a loved one or friend. That message can be as long or as short as you like, but around one minute is ideal. Then the next day listen to that message before you record another message for the next day.[10]

ADD ON

You can also record a message for your past self, revisiting a time when you felt you let yourself down or messed up or experienced trauma heartbreak. Make that message as unconditionally loving and nurturing as you can. Become your own guardian angel watching over yourself through time.

Ritual: Go with your flow

Boost your concentration.

WHY?

Mind wandering can be great for creativity, but if you need to be productive, you also need to master the art of concentration. The better your focus, the better your productivity, and the more likely your inner psychic will activate all your psychic senses at once and induce that blissful state of flow. Being productive or working hard doesn't have to feel like a chore. It can feel really, really good.

When you are in a state of flow – immersed in an activity or experience or what truly matters – you may not realize it, but you are tuning directly into your inner psychic. That's why you lose track of time, judgement, expectation and anxiety.

You may think that flow is something that just happens to you. Although that can be the case, there are ways to increase the likelihood of it happening. And one of the best ways is to use the power of daily ritual. Your brain will make associations between certain rituals and regard them as cues for your body and mind to enter a hypnotic state of flow.

HOW?

Think about those times in your life when you have lost track of time when working or doing something. What were the triggers? Once you identify them, think about them as your flow rituals.

If you don't know what they are, try this: the next time you want to be really productive or to focus better on something, drink a full glass of water or make yourself a cup of tea or coffee or whatever your favourite drink is and put your headphones on. You can play some background music – avoid songs with lyrics – or you can use ambient sounds, like waves or birdsong. Then set an alarm for thirty minutes and tell yourself if by then you still haven't been productive, you can try again tomorrow. But during those thirty minutes, make the conscious decision to concentrate fully on whatever you need to be doing.

Sometimes you just need a combination of familiar rituals, physical cues and will-power to banish apathy.

ADD ON

Remember, your inner psychic is always keen to engage you in a state of flow, because that's when you can be most creative and productive. Simple daily rituals such as making a cup of tea or setting an alarm or putting your headphones on or doing a full-body stretch or going outside for a breath of fresh air can become productivity triggers if you remember the intention behind them when you do them.

Another productivity hack is to avoid becoming overwhelmed. Don't set yourself a massive 'to do' list every morning. Choose one or two tasks and tell yourself you are going to complete them, so that when you do, you get a sense of satisfaction that will carry you along, rather than feeling you have let yourself down because you have only managed to tick one thing off your list.

SENSING AURAS

In everyday language, the word 'aura' refers to something distinctive and special about someone or something. In both science and metaphysics, it is used to describe the appearance of the invisible energy or vibration that surrounds a person, object or place.

Chances are you don't think you can see auras, but that is exactly the reason why you can't see them and why I didn't include auras in the clear-seeing chapter. You are limiting your understanding of auras to vision but, as you've now discovered, you have other psychic senses and you can use them to feel, hear or know auras.

Give this a try:

Look at someone but don't stare directly at them. Look slightly above them. Notice whatever you see, know, feel, sense, hear or understand. If any feelings, sounds, insights or shapes or colours come to mind, that is the beginning of auric vision. From that point, interpret all that comes through symbolically. For instance, if the shape is expansive and wide, this will suggest a calm state of mind, but if it is tight and sharp, this suggests tension and lack of integrity. As with your dream work, research for yourself the symbolic meaning of shapes, and do the same for any colours you sense around others. And read on ...

AURIC COLOURS

It is said there are seven colours of the rainbow in each aura and everyone has a dominant colour, but those colours will constantly change. I'm a big fan of colour therapy (chromotherapy) to boost mood, as the colours we wear and surround ourselves with have been shown[11] to impact our moods. For instance, red suggests boldness, so wear red if you need some courage. Yellow represents insight. Blue is peace, green is harmony and growth, white is purity, pink is compassion, brown is grounded, grey is organized, white is clarity, silver is sincerity, gold is wisdom, orange is creativity and purple is spiritual awakening, so you may want to surround yourself with lots of purple as you work through this book.

There isn't any colour that you should fear when sensing auras or in colour therapy, including black, which often gets a bad press when it comes to matters psychic. Black can indicate sorrow and endings, but it can also suggest mystery and hidden potential.

Sensing people's auras will take time and practice as you learn exactly how you do it – remember, you may not see them, but you may feel, hear or just understand or be aware of them. Any psychic sense is valid.

Ritual: Mirror, mirror

Look into your eyes.

WHY?
Self-knowledge is the beginning of all wisdom. How on Earth do you think you can sense the auras of others if you aren't conscious of your own?

HOW?

Every time you look into the mirror, drink in what you see. Not in a narcissistic way, but in an objective one. If you met yourself for the first time, what would you sense or feel?

If you don't like what you're sensing, smile. Smile big. Faking a smile tricks your brain into believing you are happy,[12] so smile with your mouth until your heart joins in. As you do so, imagine someone is giving you a bunch of roses or handing you an adorable puppy or kitten to hold. Notice how your eyes light up at the thought. Take a mental snapshot. That's the aura you want others to see – your inner light shining bright.

ADD ON

Always be aware of the aura you project into the world. You don't have to walk around with a permanent smile on your face, but you can sit or walk tall and your eyes can shine. The more you sense what your own aura is like, the more you will be able to sense the auras of others.

Scanning your own aura can become part of your daily routine. Think of aura-scanning in the same way as looking in a mirror before you go out to check your appearance.

If there is something that doesn't feel right when you perform an aura scan on yourself, you can adjust it. Your aura is an expression of your inner psychic and is impacted by your thoughts, feelings and actions, but you have conscious control over these. You can reshape your aura any time you want.

OTHER PSYCHIC SENSES

~~~~~~~~~~~~~~~~~~~~~~~~~~~~~~

TELEPATHY

Telepathy is the term used to describe the innate ability to sense what others are thinking and feeling, and in my opinion it is very closely linked to, or interchangeable with, clear knowing. Scientist Rupert Sheldrake popularized research into telepathy with his study of the loving therapeutic bonds between humans and their pets.[13]

CHANNELLING

'Channelling' is another term used for the ability to access information and energy in a way that is not limited by time and space. It's another word for intuition, but encompasses an awareness of your intuition being intimately connected to something outside yourself, such as a departed loved one or source energy. In my book, intuition is an inside-out job, but when your intuition is awakened, you often experience a sense of connecting to something greater than yourself, and in this blissful state inspiration flows.

Channelling has been recorded throughout history and there is evidence to suggest that it does not come from any single source. Edgar Cayce[14] was a famous trance channel in the late nineteenth and early twentieth centuries, and a number of his predictions have been verified. For the past few years, the channelling programme at IONS[15] pioneered by Dr Helané Wahbeh[16] has been demonstrating time and time again that it is possible to receive verifiable information that you could not have had access to otherwise.

MIND-BODY HEALING

Scientists are aware of the impact that your thoughts and feelings can have on your physical body. Research into the biochemical effects of the brain's functioning suggest that the cells of your body are impacted by your thoughts. This new science of epigenetics is revolutionizing our understanding of the interconnection between mind and body and has been popularized by the likes of cell biologist Dr Bruce Lipton.[17]

Stress increases heart rate and blood pressure and releases hormones that increase the risk of poor mental, emotional and physical health. So, if anxious and negative thoughts can damage your health, is it such a stretch to consider that positive and calming thoughts can heal your body? That deep breathing and relaxation techniques, like the one below, have therapeutic holistic powers?

Ritual: Deep unwind

Learn how to induce a healing state of relaxation.

WHY?
Progressive muscle relaxation is a biofeedback technique that has been shown[18] to help you destress mentally, emotionally and physically. Breathwork is highly beneficial for inducing it,[19] because breathing is something you do without thinking but can also control consciously. When you are stressed, your breathing is fast and shallow, but when you are relaxed, it is deeper and slower, so consciously slowing your breath encourages your body to relax. You have already

been introduced in previous lessons to the kind of deep breathing that your body associates with relaxation.

HOW?

Find somewhere quiet and safe to lie down. Set a timer for five or ten minutes, depending on your schedule.

Close your eyes and count backwards from ten to one. Then breathe in deeply and slowly from your stomach and through your nose and clench your hands for a few seconds.

Breathe out, fully expelling all the air in your lungs and relax your hands entirely.

Notice how much more at peace your hands feel. Experience how your hands feel. Send your hands vitality and healing.

Repeat this breathing with relaxing and releasing and noticing with healing intention how each body part feels with every part of the body in the following order: arms (flex them), shoulders (shrug them), forehead (frown), eyes (close tightly), jaw (smile broadly), chin (touch your chin to your neck), chest (expand it as you breathe in), back (arch it), buttocks (clench them), and lower legs and feet (point them).

Now your entire body is fully relaxed, stay still and notice your rate and depth of breathing. With every inhalation, feel calm and peace flow into you, and with every exhalation, feel stress and tension flow away from your body. Tell yourself to unwind and find inner calm and carry on doing this until the timer goes off.

ADD ON

The more you do this ritual, the easier it will be for you to consciously choose to relax and send yourself deep healing whenever you feel tension rising.

If you are short of time or need to feel instantly calm, simply breathe in deeply, and as you do so, tense your entire body for a few seconds. Then breathe out and let all the tension go.

ENERGY HEALING

Energy healing[20] involves the use of energy, including thoughts, to heal emotionally and/or physically. It could be said to be a form of prayer. One form of it is known as Reiki. A 2020 study[21] by the IONS looked at energy healing and its effects on pain and reported very promising results. Other studies[22] on the power of intention have reported slight benefits from prayer and blessings.

Can your thoughts or intentions truly heal? Sometimes. Your thoughts can influence nerve connections all over your body, but as well as the focus and dedication required, there are other factors to take into consideration, such as the time of diagnosis.

Mind–body self-healing should never exclude conventional medicine, but there is an emerging trend within medical practice to include the healing power of the spiritual. In the words of neurologist and critical care specialist Dr Adam Rizvi,[23] who offers teachings that blend spiritual and scientific rigour, 'Disease is a doorway, an opportunity for growth. We're being called to transform.' Rizvi's passion[24] is to help us remember what it is to be whole and know that we are innately perfect, as this redefines our approach to health and healing.

The best approach is holistic[25] – alternative therapies, such as energy healing, medical intuition, homoeopathy, herbalism,[26] etc., *alongside* conventional medicine such as drugs.

And it really is important to not confuse physical well-being with psychic or soul health. As you get older, your body is going to go through changes outside your control, regardless of how many healing thoughts you send it. Do all you can to nourish and take loving care of your body as the temple of your soul, but know that it's your soul's health that matters most. In the words of Tolkien, 'It is not the strength of the body, but the strength of the spirit.'

And continuing this line of thought, if your mind can influence your body, surely your body can influence your mind? Of course it can. It has been shown[27] that your brain is led by your daily actions. That's why there is so much emphasis on daily rituals in this programme.

WARP SPEED AHEAD

Your psychic senses are all interconnected. There will be significant cross-over. They work synergistically.

That's why, although some of the rituals in this programme appear to focus on igniting one particular psychic sense, each has the power to activate and empower all of them. And be aware too that the more you fire up the psychic energy within you, the more likely you are to connect to the invisible energies *around* you. Don't be surprised at this stage in your psychic empowerment and personal growth[28] if you notice more coincidences and have more vivid dreams, spontaneous intuitions, and so on.

From time to time, though, psychic blocks happen to everyone, even those who consider themselves sensitive.

FAQ: 'I'm just not receiving any psychic information and have no idea what my psychic receptor sense is. I'm wondering how to get over this block?'

Just relax. Simply let your inner psychic know you believe it is working quietly behind the scenes on your behalf and it will speak to you when you are ready. Continue your daily psychic empowerment rituals. The worst thing you can do right now is force or strain for an outcome. The more you do that, the message you are sending to your inner psychic is that you don't trust it.

The ideal mental state for psychic reception is a relaxed and gently focused one – the mental state that daily breathwork and relaxation can help you achieve.

Chances are this psychic block is happening because your waking life is overwhelming. The demands of the material world, along with a large dose of accompanying stress, are drowning out the voice of your inner psychic. You may also not yet be ready to let go of your need to control outcomes in your waking life. The most receptive state for empowering your inner psychic is to let go of any expectations of control.

Remind yourself that you will make smarter decisions if you take a step back and give your intuition a chance. A sign you are getting closer to connecting with your intuition is that you feel comfortable in your own company. Indeed, spending time alone is a joy.

There can be no better catalyst for psychic empowerment than solitary daily meditation, so if you are struggling to develop your sensitivity, give it priority. Remember too that any dream recall is a sign of inner psychic awakening, so make writing down your dreams every day a sacred act and move forward from there.

If you still aren't sure which is the optimum way for your inner psychic to speak to you, or how your psychic awareness is most likely to break through, a simple way to find out is to think about how you relax or what you like to do during your down time. If you adore beautiful scenery and spending time in nature, chances are clear seeing is your optimum route or the best starting point. If you relax best by organizing, tidying up, exercising and keeping yourself occupied, my guess is you are a clear hearer and may have a breakthrough here first. If you are drawn to chilling out and doing nothing in particular, clear sensing will very likely be your first psychic love. And if you are the kind of person who loves variety and socializing, then clear knowing is likely to be your psychic superpower.

This isn't a science, but it might offer an indication of where to direct your focus initially. If it doesn't, perhaps you are someone who doesn't have a dominant psychic sense and you can juggle them all. Indeed, merging your psychic senses can be a catalyst for growth.

SYNAESTHESIA

Synaesthesia is a mysterious condition that occurs when one of your senses triggers sensations, images or experience in another sense. This trait[29] is more common in artists, poets, painters and highly creative people, including psychics who sense auras. So, if colours had sounds, what would they be? If words had a taste, what would they taste like? If sounds could be seen, what would they look like? If smells could be felt, what would they feel like? If you are facing a block, or even if you aren't, give merging a try and see what manifests.

Don't forget too that your *trust* is everything. If you believe in your own psychic powers, or at the very least are open to them, it is easier for your inner psychic to grow in power. If you aren't quite there yet, that's okay; just repeatedly tell yourself you are already psychic. You have the power of your will. Use the proven power of affirmation – your will – until your self-belief catches up and your inner psychic defines you.

ON YOUR WAY

If you have been performing the suggested rituals every day for at least three weeks, you may already be noticing some strange – unfamiliar, not weird – things happening. The experience will be different for each one of you, but here are some clear signs that your inner psychic is becoming empowered. You may not experience all of them, and some may still be a work in progress, but experiencing any of these is a power point:

- ⊙ Dream recall, alongside awareness of just how much your dreams can comment on and influence your waking life.
- ⊙ Noticing how your eyes shine when you have your photo taken or look in the mirror.
- ⊙ Taking yourself much less seriously and finding laughter[30] comes naturally.
- ⊙ Finding it easier to forgive others as well as yourself for any mistakes made.
- ⊙ Finding it impossible not to be authentic[31] and speak your truth,[32] even if it isn't what others want to hear.
- ⊙ Noticing things more and marvelling at the number of coincidences[33] in your life.
- ⊙ Focusing on what people do, not what they say or think.
- ⊙ Finding that things that used to bother or upset you just don't anymore.
- ⊙ Not needing other people to get you because you understand that the only person who needs to get you is *you*.
- ⊙ Finding that your growing self-awareness and self-sufficiency leads to the loss of friends or colleagues who are no longer in energetic alignment with you. Your phone beeps less and you are happy when it is silent. Quality, not quantity, matters more to you now in all your relationships.[34]
- ⊙ Looking for similarities and connections between yourself and others. This feeling of interconnection means you never feel alone,[35] even when you are alone.
- ⊙ Understanding that emotional pain is a clear sign you are not in alignment with your soul.
- ⊙ Seeing crisis[36] and trauma[37] as opportunities to evolve. Like a kettle boiling, being ready to reset and release things that are no longer serving you.

☾ Realizing the destination matters less and less to you, because
   you are focused on feeling blissful and fulfilled in the present.
☾ Feeling more regularly drawn to nature and animals.

You'll notice that with the exception of dream recall, none of these
signs mentions psychic buzzwords like 'auras' or 'visions' or 'telepathy'. That's because these buzzwords are window dressing. They
truly are not what being 'psychic' actually means.

Above all, as you awaken your inner psychic, you'll start feeling
more comfortable outside your comfort zone. Fitting in or doing
what is expected just isn't your priority anymore. The aim of this
book isn't to make you feel comfortable. In fact, I hope as you read
each chapter at times you feel inexplicably restless, uncertain even.
The point being made over and over again in your training is that
outside yourself isn't the place to find fulfilment. The aim of this
programme is to kick-start your incredible voyage within and your
inner psychic, like this book, is always pulling your attention
toward your inner world, because that is where everything starts
and ends. If you are calm and positive from within, you are trans-
mitting the perfect energy signal for success in the external world.

And you can make that inner psychic shift anytime you like. In
an instant. Let's do it right now. Consciously tell yourself you
deserve happiness. Pour all your belief and trust into it. Then dive
back into your life in the certain knowledge that your inner psychic
is now primed.

MOVING ON

Let's keep the momentum going now. Armed with self-belief, purpose and positivity, and an ever-growing awareness of the full range of your inner psychic senses and the optimum ways you can tap into them, you are more than ready to become your own oracle.

Become your Own Oracle

This book was inspired by a 'Be your Own Psychic' item I was asked to do for *This Morning*, a much-loved British TV news and entertainment show[1] in 2021. The producers knew about my collaboration with scientists researching the psychic potential within us all, as well as my desire to bring regulation into the booming psychic services industry. In 2019 this industry was estimated to reach a staggering 2.2 billion dollars and it has grown considerably since then, due to the crisis and uncertainty of the pandemic.

While there is no doubt that there are ethical psychics out there who may be able to tap into your energy and offer you healing advice, there is no denying that there are also countless frauds[2] and spiritual narcissists, some with cult-like followings,[3] who should be avoided at all costs.

There is also no denying that science is proving that by far the best person to offer you intuitive advice or to glimpse your future is your very own inner psychic. Not enough people know about that latest scientific development and they continue to seek out professional psychics. I'm making it my mission to mainstream this emerging science of consciousness and make reliance on intermediaries the exception rather than the rule.

A LONG AND WINDING ROAD

Born into a family of psychics and Spiritualists, I was surrounded by people who could sense beyond the material and connect to the unseen world of dreams, spirit and the afterlife. However, despite my upbringing and confident belief in the psychic world, I never felt confident of my own psychic gifts. I did have moments of profound intuition and mesmerizing dreams, but they never felt extraordinary or evidence 'enough'.

I signed up for psychic course after course, had reading after reading with spiritual experts, burnt the midnight oil reading esoteric book after book – wrote some of them too. I meditated, went on yoga retreats, affirmed, visualized, journaled, tried hypnosis, hypnotherapy, the Tarot, crystals, astrology, numerology and every ology and psychic development course imaginable. If it was out there, I was all over it. I was searching for the solution, the perfect teacher. Some teachers or courses spoke to me more than others. Some of the techniques I learned felt insightful. And some of the research I uncovered led to light-bulb moments. But I was looking for a mentor to hold my hand. I didn't get that becoming psychic was *my* job. Intuition can never be discovered 'out there' or through others. It has to be found within.

Of course we can all learn from others, and wise teachers are a much-needed blessing. There is tremendous value in having mentors to guide you, but there must come a time when you have the courage to trust your own judgement. If you constantly defer to others, your inner psychic doesn't stand a chance. It is virtually impossible to empower it if you are addicted to validation from others.

The journey to self-trust is the journey not just of becoming your own psychic, but the biggest challenge of anyone's life. Some people find this journey easier than others, and if you were born into a loving and supportive family who fostered your self-belief from the get go, you do have a head start. Most of us, though, myself included, didn't get that head start. However, low self-esteem isn't necessarily a disadvantage, because the psychic growth potential of outgrowing it is huge. Sometimes if a person's life is too easy there is no incentive for personal growth and, to risk repeating myself, the meaning of our lives is to evolve.

Success and happiness are rarely found in your comfort zone and you tend to find your meaning on the paths you try to avoid. If you have never experienced crises and setbacks, you won't gain the wisdom from overcoming them. So, for those of us who suffer from lack of self-belief, a good starting-point is to think of your inner fragility as an incredible opportunity to reset and fast-track your psychic growth. After all, it is only through the cracks that the light can come in. If you let another person tell you the way forward when you feel uncertain, you are denying yourself a remarkable leap in psychic growth.

I spent far too many years of my life searching outside myself and asking others for solutions which could only offer solace by papering over my low self-esteem. Looking within was alarming because I wasn't sure I could deal with what I found there or what I didn't find there. It felt like leaping into a black hole. But, trust me, when you do take that leap of faith, you won't ever look back. I hope this chapter in particular will give you the courage you need to finally turn your external-focused eyes into internal ones.

It wasn't a teacher, guru, book, video, Tarot card or any kind of reading or course that helped me let go of what was holding me back. It was what many might consider to be the nemesis of psychic development – the world of science.

It was the earnest desire to offer something more tangible to my readers than 'just believe' that was the breakthrough. I found a whole new world of scientists out there busy researching consciousness and the transformative power of the inner world. I discovered that sixth sense is in our DNA and that there are simple things we can do to connect directly to our intuition. Hence this book.

As the introduction and Lesson One made clear, the science of consciousness matters even if you feel it is 'boring', because if the voices of fear and doubt creep in (and they will), you can be reassured that some enlightened scientists are normalizing psychic abilities, taking them seriously and offering undeniable evidence the inner psychic is real. And if science is willing to consider this leap of faith, so can you.

REACHING OUT

If at this stage in the programme you still strongly feel the need to visit a psychic, medium or fortune-teller because you think they have superior or special powers compared to you, please reread lessons one to five carefully.

There is no harm if a visit to a psychic is occasional, doesn't cost too much and gives you a different perspective – we all need that sometimes – but repeat visits are to be avoided. Any kind of dependency diminishes the true power of your inner psychic. And if that psychic tells you what they think you should do, a pinch of salt please. Always make your own mind up before following the advice of others, however blessed you think they may be. *Certainly, take on board their insights, but a great teacher will always encourage you to be independent and to be the pilot of your own life.*

You have to understand that psychics are not trained counsellors. If you feel emotionally vulnerable, visit a qualified therapist or counsellor,[4] or talk to your GP rather than someone who claims to have psychic gifts or expertise in divination or 'fortune-telling'.

PROPS

And just as psychics, mediums and spiritual teachers won't empower your inner psychic – only you can do that – when it comes to divination systems and psychic tools, like astrology and crystals, etc., there's no true power in them either. The magic isn't in *them*, it is in *you* and in your understanding of and belief in them.

For example, perhaps you have always thought Tarot cards have mystical powers or that astrology[5] determines your fate. It's easy to understand why you may have these beliefs. Horror movies have a lot to do with it. After *The Omen* movies came out, for example, Ouija boards became something to fear for no good reason.

Without exception, the only reason divination systems or tools can sometimes feel so accurate or insightful is because your inner psychic seizes on them as props to help you focus your own incredible intuitive energy.

If you believe in the power of Tarot cards more than your own intuitive power, you have to ask yourself what message this is sending to your inner psychic. A pack of illustrated cards is more influential or knows more about you than you? It's not really an empowering message, is it?

This isn't to say you shouldn't ever use psychic props. Quite the contrary – as long as you are fully aware that they are simply props and any insights or healing (as well as fears and uncertainties) originate from you and not them, they can be helpful modalities that give your inner psychic work structure. That's why this lesson is going to encourage you to become an expert in the use of one psychic tool or system.

TAKE ONE

In the resources you will find an 'Inner Psychic Tools A to Z' (*page 245*), offering you an overview of the most readily available tools professional psychics or spiritual teachers (also known as light-workers) use for readings, healings, courses, workshops, etc. Some you may already be familiar with, others less so, but be sure to read the entire list mindfully. Then select one or two systems your inner psychic feels most in tune with. Trust your first impressions here.

(If there is one you have detailed knowledge or experience of already, in the spirit of adventure set it aside for now. Time to try something new.)

Then on a piece of blank paper write down the names of the one or two systems or tools that resonate. As you write them, say them out loud. Notice how your body reacts to each word. Notice how your voice sounds when you say each one. What feels right? What trips off your tongue? If each system was a colour, what would it be? If each system was a shape, what would that shape be?

Go for the system that resonates best for you on an invisible psychic level. Then in the coming hours or days, become an in-depth psychical researcher of it. Invest time in learning as much as you can about it and how and why it works.

If you are interested in the science and psychology behind that system, see what you can find out in research journals. If there is very little out there, what does this suggest to you, given your newfound knowledge about spiritual science and how alive it currently is?

Of course you may prefer to simply look at the fascinating history or myths and legends associated with the system. There's always going to be a book or course about whatever system you choose and stacks of free online material.

Whatever approach you choose, the only rule is not to over-invest your funds and to keep researching in your own way and your own time, until you understand enough to do simple readings for yourself.

Remain cautious as you investigate. There's a lot of false information out there. Just because someone says something is true, however much of an authority on the subject they may seem, that does not make it so. Apply your questioning mind to everything. Even if you are presented with 'facts', take them on board and absorb what resonates, but let your feelings or sense about those facts inform you. If you feel inspired and want to know more and more, that's a big clue you are headed in the right direction.

Note: I'm hoping you will also seriously question everything I have thrown at you so far in this book. I'd be delighted if you disagree, because it is a sure-fire sign your inner psychic is alive. Scepticism is the mark of a great mind.

Ritual: Your everyday oracle

Give yourself a reading.

WHY?
The fact that many of these systems are so ancient and yet still in use today testifies to their ability to trigger deep

insights and empower those who use them. However, you don't need someone else to use them for you. Not one of the systems is so complicated that you can't learn it yourself. Indeed, most of the so-called self-proclaimed psychic or intuitive experts in those systems are self-taught.

HOW?

Every day for at least a week, be sure to consult your chosen oracle and do a reading for yourself.

You can use it to gain advice or insight about a specific issue or you can use it to see a potential future. However you decide to use it, never forget that it is not the system that has the power but the energy and belief you bring to it.

Record in a journal any insights that come to you as a result of using your chosen system. And if you are using your system as a predictive tool and some of the things it predicts turn out to be true, again remember what your inner psychic programme training so far has taught you: the future isn't written in stone. Any future reading offers you a glimpse of a potential future, but you can change your future by the decisions you make in the present. In this sense, you are always your own oracle, creating your future in every moment, with every thought, feeling and action you take.

When your oracle research period is up, consider how helpful it has been. Did your prop offer useful guidance or correctly predict your future? If so, by all means carry on using it every day as a way of empowering your inner psychic. It's a method that works for you, so celebrate that. You may also want to do some free readings for people you know.

However, be sure to also consider if using your system has been as helpful or as immediate as your daily dream decoding or your newfound awareness of the many wonderful invisible ways your inner psychic speaks to you.

If it hasn't been that helpful, you can experiment with other systems, or you can simply ditch unnecessary props and trust in the power of your inner psychic to connect to you directly.

QUESTION TIME

Since asking questions[6] – and understanding that there can be many answers to the same question and every answer has its limitations and the most important part of asking is the insights you formulate in response – has been a theme of this chapter, and indeed this book, this feels like the perfect opportunity to place some other frequently asked psychic questions.

Q: 'SHOULD I EVER VISIT A PSYCHIC?'

No. Every time you visit a psychic you weaken your trust in your own inner psychic. Indeed, using your psychic powers in times of crisis and emergency is one of the most powerful ways to empower them. If you go to someone else during these times, you are depriving yourself of that serious confidence boost.

If, however, you really do feel the need to visit a psychic, be sure to use the meeting as information gathering only. Please trust your own instincts above those of a stranger, however many endorsements they have from people you know, or however charismatic, wise and sincere they seem to be.

And if you don't feel clear responses are coming through and the psychic doesn't make you feel confident and uplifted about yourself, avoid them.

Finally, please make your visit a one-off. Dependency is a sure-fire way to silence your inner psychic and diminish your self-worth.

See also the advice for visiting mediums and psychics (page 257).

Q: 'HOW CAN WE HELP CHILDREN TRUST IN THEIR INNER PSYCHIC?'

Start with yourself. Children are natural copycats. If you trust your own inner psychic, chances are your children will trust it too. Encourage them not to discount the value of their hunches and their dreams, and let them know there is power in sending loving thoughts. Make the expression of feelings a good thing to practise. And when they are old enough, work through the first four lessons in this book with them. Teach them what you have learned about your inner psychic there.

Above all, let them be. Children for the most part are naturally sensitive, spontaneous, intuitive and creative. If you see them daydreaming or drifting away into a make-believe world with a make-believe friend, don't interfere. Encourage them to tell you their night-time dreams and to trust in their own magic.

Q: 'CAN MY PSYCHIC POWERS BE USED TO CONTROL OTHERS?'

No. If you have a desire to control others using your psychic powers, you have not discovered any psychic powers. What you have discovered is your own lack of self-worth. When your inner psychic is empowered, you don't have any desire to control others. The only person you want to influence and mould is yourself.

In much the same way, nobody can control you psychically. It may be true that others can influence you using the power of suggestion, and you may sense when someone is thinking about you in a positive or negative way, but there is absolutely no way you can be made to do anything that you are not in agreement with. Hypnosis can't even get you to do what you aren't already open to.

If you have heard the term 'psychic attack', know that it's an oxymoron. Nobody can attack your inner psychic without your consent. You are not a helpless victim. Empowering your inner psychic encourages you to create boundaries, practise self-care and trust in your own powers. If you are highly suggestible and feel vulnerable to attack from others, this is a clear sign you need to go back to basics and start from Lesson One again. Your inner psychic needs much more loving attention from you.

Q: 'HOW DO PSYCHIC POWERS AND WITCHCRAFT DIFFER?'

Witchcraft is an ancient system that uses spells, rituals and other magical tools and techniques to help change or influence the natural or elemental energies of the universe. In other words, energy from the outside is internalized and used for personal and collective well-being. It is often confused with Wicca, but Wicca falls into the category of neo-paganism, which is a nature-based religion with pre-Christian roots.

Psychics use the power of ritual too, but they understand that while tools can make it easier to ignite their psychic ability, everything they need is already within them. Internal emotional and psychological shifts and sensing abilities beyond the five senses are prioritized. So it's inside out, rather than outside in.

Having said that, many witches choose to be psychic, just as you can choose to be religious and psychic.

INTO YOUR UNKNOWN

All the lessons so far have been designed to help you tune into your inner psychic not through forcing or straining, or relying on props or gurus, but through noticing and observing your own impressions and understanding that your real power is separate from not only your body and mind, and also your thoughts and feelings.

Your inner psychic is quite simply the unlimited creative potential within you. You could call it your consciousness, your essence, your intuition or your soul. Better still, call it *you*.

The more aware you become of your true non-physical self, the easier it becomes to tune out the distractions and limitations of the material world. It also becomes easier to connect to a sense of yourself as unlimited potential where anything is possible.

So, in that spirit of inner possibility are you ready for one giant leap forward?

LIGHT YEARS AHEAD

Most of us believe we have a soul, as well as a body and mind, but at this point in your programme, you need to go way beyond that belief.

A soul isn't something you own or which belongs to you. It's not even a wildly creative part of you that you can tap into. I've used this 'tune or tap into a part of yourself' language up until this point simply because it is familiar and can help you adjust to your spiritual nature, and the inner psychic handshake ritual (*see page 70*) is something you can still do every day, but from now on I want to encourage you to do it with the awareness that you are a soul with a body, not a body with a soul.

You have a body, you have a mind, but you don't have a soul. You *are* soul. Your inner psychic is the real *you*.

To quote Shakespeare, 'This above all, to thine own self be true.' Thinking of yourself as a soul in physical form, you instantly expand your awareness beyond your body and the material world. It's not a lonely or isolating experience. It doesn't cut you off from the material world, it deepens your unique and intimate connection with it. What is within you connects to what is around you.

Once you trust your inner psychic and complete yourself rather than seeking that completion outside yourself, you feel whole and at peace. And from this place of inner calm you naturally notice connections between yourself and others. Empathy is your natural state. You realize that your soul energy is not just individual but is also interconnected with the energy of everyone and everything. And in that realization your consciousness blends with the energy of the entire universe.

You may already have felt this sense of blissful oneness and interconnection when you have spent time in nature, or fallen in love, or been so engrossed in doing something that you've forgotten about time and your physical needs. It is often called a peak or bliss or flow or channelled experience. You are fully experiencing your awareness of yourself as soul.

OUT OF YOUR MIND?

Any discussion of your non-physical essence inevitably begs the question of whether or not your consciousness can exist independently of your body and mind. Can your inner psychic disengage from your body and mind?

You could say every time you fall asleep and dream or whenever you visualize or meditate or remember someone or something important to you, your inner psychic is travelling somewhere beyond the material.

Perhaps you have encountered mystics who claim to be able to astral travel or go out of body during meditation, trance or when dreaming. This can trigger false fears of your soul getting trapped or lost, but as long as your heart is beating, your consciousness can never lose its attachment to your body. However, when your heart finally stops beating, there is tentative evidence to suggest that it can *perhaps* continue to exist independent of your body and mind. And the very real possibility of an afterlife or spirit world, and how you can become your own medium too, is the final fantasy or frontier coming up next ...

'The grey rain curtain of this world rolls back, and all turns to silver glass and then you see it ... White Shores and beyond, a far green country under a swift sunrise.'

Gandalf, *Lord of the Rings*

Become your Own Medium

You are not your body. You are not even your mind.

Once you become aware of the non-physical nature of your inner psychic or consciousness, the concept of there being an afterlife really doesn't seem such a stretch. And given that quantum science suggests everything is energy, and energy is infinite, is it such a leap to think that your consciousness, that spark of life within you, may survive bodily death?

Indeed, whenever there is talk about being psychic, talk about communicating with the other side, and the spirits, angels and spiritual beings that may or may not inhabit this higher state of consciousness, AKA the afterlife, is never far behind.

You may also begin to wonder why on Earth you spend so much time concerned with material or temporary things when all of them will disappear when you die. Far better surely to focus on what is eternal – the love, compassion and deep understanding that never dies. Far better to empower your inner medium.

MEDIUMSHIP

The term for communicating with the afterlife is 'mediumship', and a 'medium'[1] is someone who receives messages from the other side. Many people confuse psychics and mediums, but they aren't the same, even though many psychics are also mediums and many mediums[2] are also psychic.[3]

A psychic is someone who senses or knows unseen things in this life; a medium is someone who allegedly offers 'proof' of the soul's survival after death by connecting to departed spirits and the afterlife and offering the sitter information that they can't possibly know unless it comes from the departed loved ones.

And guess what? You don't need to visit a medium to get proof of the afterlife[4] either. Just as you can be your own psychic, you can become your own medium too. The final lesson of your inner psychic programme is going to unravel how. First, though, let's re-introduce you to some compelling and always surprising afterlife statistics and science.

THE AFTERLIFE IS REAL?

Surveys[5] repeatedly show that even though religion[6] and belief in God are on the decline, up to 70 per cent of us still believe in some kind of an afterlife. That's a majority, so once again I'm likely to be speaking to the converted here. And the staggering thing is that to date there is no definitive proof to back up this majority belief.

Even though sceptics rightly point out this lack of absolute proof of an afterlife, it is important to point out that there is no absolute proof that heaven doesn't exist either. However, there is something that may come as close to proof as we're likely to get of consciousness carrying on after death, and that is near-death experience (NDE).

One of the most famous examples of an NDE is that of Dr Eben Alexander,[7] a neurosurgeon who didn't believe in the afterlife until he had a near-death experience and came back utterly transformed. Anita Moorjani[8] and David Ditchfield[9] are other noted people who have written bestselling books about their NDEs. Alongside these, however, are numerous people who haven't written bestselling books about their NDEs but have also found that their whole attitude to life changed afterwards. The transformative power of NDEs is perhaps one of the strongest arguments for their authenticity.

Steve's story:

Yes, I 'died' on the operating table, for three minutes forty seconds to be precise. Yes, I saw myself on that table. Yes, I was drawn into a tunnel of light and saw my life again, but all that, however, pales in comparison to the sense of deep peace I felt. I used to be suspicious of people who smiled a lot, but now I can't stop smiling. I used to be such an anxious person, always worried about something or someone. I used to worry about my job, what car I drove, what I looked like, what people thought about me, who I spent time with and all those things that I know don't matter. I'm happy to smile at anyone and everything now, because I know that the only thing I will be evaluated on is how much I have felt love and how much I have loved. I also know that everyone is capable of love and deserves to be loved and that we are all connected in spirit.

NDEs have some interesting research[10] behind them, most notably Dr Parnia's 2014 NDE study, which suggests consciousness can survive body and brain death for at least a minute or so after death.

Alongside Dr Parnia, other medical pioneers also studying near-death experiences scientifically, such as Dr Pim van Lommel, can find no definitive medical explanation for them. Hallucination typically causes depression and confusion, but those who experience

NDEs often return to their lives with a newfound meaning and purpose.

Due to advances in resuscitation techniques, more and more people are brought back from the brink, and contributing to a steadily growing collection of NDE stories, with most showing remarkable and unexplained consistencies, despite differences in the experiencers' age, beliefs and culture.

Alongside promising NDE research and enlightening new studies[11] into what happens to the dying brain – strong indications of vivid memory recall – bear in mind that survival of consciousness studies take place all year round at parapsychology departments in universities and psychic research organizations all over the globe. There are also independent organizations such as the Galileo Commission,[12] founded by David Lorimer,[13] and psychologist Gary Schwartz's Soulphone[14] foundation technology. I also want to appreciatively mention the underground community of paranormal investigators (ghost hunters) who scientifically investigate reports of afterlife activity every day.

A brief note about ghosts

In traditional thinking, the difference between ghosts and spirits is that ghosts aren't aware they have passed.

Hauntings require a book of their own (you may want to check out my HarperCollins titles *Ghosts and Hauntings* and *The Psychic World A to Z*) and there is a great deal of credible research[15] and scepticism[16] out there, but I am going to briefly reference[17] ghost hunter Loyd Auerbach, a legend in the paranormal community, here. He investigates the scenes of alleged hauntings and once he has eliminated all logical explanations, he says he just cannot rule out the chance that paranormal phenomena might be happening.

Auerbach isn't alone in his findings, and if you are interested in finding out more, you will discover many ghost-hunting enthusiasts out there, many using technology and science-based testing. If you get a chance, you might want to take part in a ghost hunt yourself. Indeed, anything that encourages an open-minded approach to the idea that consciousness may survive bodily death is nutrition for your inner psychic.

Be sure, though, to approach it in a light-hearted, positive and sceptical way and always remember that nothing you experience can harm you, because when it comes to understanding the afterlife,[18] fear and love cannot exist at the same time.

PARTING VISIONS

Parting visions,[19] where someone who is dying sees visions of departed loved ones, spirits and angels, stand alongside NDEs as potential proof of an afterlife, because in the majority of instances the dying person is not hallucinating or in a medically induced altered mental state. In addition, although some of these accounts are from the people who are crossing over themselves, others are hugely persuasive as they are experienced by relatives or friends or even doctors and nurses caring for the dying.

Sceptics argue that deathbed visions are a natural tranquillizer to ease the shock and fear of the dying brain, but this can't fully explain the comfort and strength they bring both those who are dying and their loved ones. I have experience of working in hospice care[20] and being with a dying person when they pass. When a person dies, it's clear their spark or essence has gone and the body has the feel of discarded clothes. Sometimes there are blissful moments before passing that range from something as simple as a smile to a temporary return of lucidity. These moments offer a glimpse of the soul's infinity and beauty in the most tired and aged of bodies.

THERE AND BACK AGAIN

Given that modern physics suggests that everything is made up of energy, your body is energy, as are your thoughts and feelings. So is it such a stretch to consider the possibility that when you die, the energy of your consciousness or inner psychic can survive in an unseen dimension? And is it unreasonable to ponder that it might just be possible for you to tune into that unseen eternal energy?

It was a revelation to me to discover just how seriously the scientific community is beginning to take the possibility of an afterlife and just how much research is being done. In 2016 the American Psychological Association published a groundbreaking book called *Transcendent Mind*, co-authored by Dr Mossbridge (who happens to be my *Premonition Code* co-author too), which offers a powerful argument that consciousness may be able to exist separate from body and mind. If this is possible, it certainly offers a workable explanation for NDEs, out of body experiences, parting visions and even past-life recall.[21]

Once you have opened your mind to the possibility that there might be an afterlife, the most empowering way for you to connect to it is not indirectly through a medium, but directly.

HEAVEN IS CALLING YOU

I get countless messages from people asking me why they can't sense a departed loved one or how to see afterlife signs. I tell them that the issue is not with the spirit world, as departed loved ones can reach out to us at any time, the issue is with us. First there needs to be an acceptance of someone's physical passing.

The pain of grief[22] is excruciating. There is no right and wrong way to grieve, but it is essential you give yourself love and self-care as you let your feelings out. It is okay to scream. It is okay to feel angry. It is okay to cry. Not all tears are an evil. Tears are cathartic and healing. You are not losing control or going mad. You are reacting to loss.

It's likely that you have heard of the stages of grief[23] – denial, anger, bargaining, sadness and acceptance – but there is no one-size-fits-all way to grieve. You find yourself experiencing feelings you never knew you had. The 'Time heals' advice isn't comforting. You don't forget a loved one; you adapt to their loss. You are no longer the same person.[24] Your loss is now a part of who you are, and the grief journey[25] is to reach a place when you can think of the person who has gone with a smile before a tear. You have a clear choice now. Your life has changed forever. Are you going to make this change a positive or a negative one? What better memorial to a departed loved one's life than remembering them with joy and living your life to the full in their honour?

Loving deeply in the face of impermanence[26] is always a risk worth taking. If you have ever lost a loved one, you will know that they are somehow still with you, alive in your memories, dreams and heart. Moving beyond grief means being able to remember them without crippling pain. It is also a deep inner knowing that whenever you remember them with love, see them with your inner eyes, dream about them or sense them around you, they are alive within and around you. Grief can be a mighty inner psychic awakening.

Again, I must stress this deep afterlife[27] connection won't happen overnight. Take all the time you need to grieve fully, but know that true love is love that can set a spirit free. When a loved one dies, amid all the pain they give you an opportunity to reclaim part of yourself that you gave away. So, if you give yourself plenty of time to adjust and plenty of self-love following a bereavement, you will in time find that your inner strength and potential are renewed.

SIGNS

And I do want to bring to your attention here the many stories[28] and messages I have had the privilege to receive from people who say how much comfort afterlife[29] signs give them, as they would give anything to spend a few more moments on Earth with departed loved ones. These signs[30] give them tremendous hope that perhaps one day they will be united in spirit. The most moving stories are sometimes from those who had no idea their loved one – or pet – was going to die, as they passed suddenly.[31] They are a reminder that every moment you spend with people you care about is a priceless gift.

Whether you are in the midst of grief or not, the rituals below will help you get to that peaceful place – perhaps the sixth stage of grief – by showing you that at any moment you can connect to a loved one in spirit. Your inner psychic can keep them forever alive in your heart and remind you that grief is but the darkness before the dawn and death is a journey that we all must take; it ends a life, but not a relationship.

Ritual: Mirror gazing

Connect to the spirit of a departed loved one.

WHY?
Mirror gazing is a powerful ritual inspired by a technique that dates back to ancient Greece, where people would visit temples devoted to the dead and undergo a series of lengthy rituals in order to contact spirits.

HOW?
You can recreate this ancient practice for modern times in the comfort of your own home. But you should perhaps not do it in the first few months following a bereavement, as your emotions will be too raw, and calm non-expectation is needed.

All you need is a mirror, a comfortable chair and some peace and alone time at twilight.

Sit in your chair, making sure there is light behind you. Then place the mirror in front of you in such a way that you can gaze into it but not actually see your own reflection. You could perhaps lean it against a wall or place it on a table in front of you.

Take some deep breaths and in your own time enter a relaxed, meditative state. Make memories of your departed loved one the focus of your meditation. Ensure that the memories are ones that bring you joy or make you smile.

Keep reflecting on your departed loved one and gazing into the mirror and see what visions or sensations appear either in the mirror or in your mind's eye. If nothing seems to come through, enjoy the feelings of love for your departed loved one and trust that in coming days contact with them will be made through your dreams or through afterlife signs.

It is important to perform this ritual as often as you can and to keep a record of any impressions or visions that come through. Dr Raymond Moody, who coined the term 'near-death experience', reports over 80 per cent success rate with it among his clients.[32]

DIRECT MEDIUMSHIP

The most powerful and immediate way to connect to a departed loved one is to think about them with feelings of love and gratitude. Mirror gazing is a way to do that, but you can do this anytime, anywhere. You can simply talk to loved ones in your mind. You can also dream about them. When people write to me asking why they haven't experienced an afterlife sign, I tell them to look to their dreams.

If a departed loved one has appeared to you in your dreams, you may dismiss the dream as just part of the grieving process or wishful thinking, but when a person is grieving, the emotions are typically painful and conflicting, increasing the likelihood that such a dream visitation may be an afterlife sign. Research[33] shows that in over 88 per cent of cases, dreaming about a departed loved one eases the grieving process, and that is heaven sent in my book.

DEATH IS BUT A DREAM

Some ancient cultures believed the dream state was a door to the afterlife. That belief lingers to this day. Hallmarks of afterlife dreams are their vivid and realistic feel. They are also impossible to forget on waking and you may be able to remember them for days, weeks or even years afterwards. You don't know how or why, but on waking you know that this was more than a symbolic dream. Visitation dreams have a heightened sense of clarity and reality that you can somehow feel, touch and sense. Symbolic dreams, by contrast, feel like fragments, are easily forgotten and have a shifting, surreal, random style.

In a visitation dream, the departed loved one appears in a realistic or natural setting, such as the dreamer's bedroom or a park, and talks or gazes lovingly at the dreamer. It's as if the person is alive again in the dream with all their mannerisms.

Night visitations are the perfect way for spirits of departed loved ones to connect to you without causing unhelpful alarm. With the benefit of hindsight, I can see clearly that when I lost my mother and longed for a dramatic afterlife sign, dreaming vividly of her was absolutely the most healing afterlife connection for me. I wasn't ready for anything else.

If departed loved ones appear in your dreams, celebrate those dreams as the afterlife signs they are. If, however, departed loved ones have not yet entered your dreams, you can try incubating an afterlife dream.

Ritual: Incubating an afterlife dream

Reconnect with a departed loved one.

WHY?
Apart from the joy of seeing them again and spending time with them, if there were things you never got to say, dreams offer you an opportunity to talk to them again and keep that relationship alive in spirit.

HOW?
Simply set the intention before you go to sleep to dream about your departed loved one by remembering or visualizing.

ADD ON
As with all your psychic empowerment work, if this afterlife dream incubation doesn't work, trust that your inner psychic knows best. Release expectation. Continue to think of someone you have lost and loved with tenderness and gratitude. Talk to them in your mind and heart. Perhaps they will speak to you through the phenomenon of afterlife signs.

AFTERLIFE SIGNS

A rainbow appears when you think of a departed loved one, or a white feather in an unexpected place brings you comfort when you feel scared or alone. Or you hear a song on the radio that has strong personal associations with someone in spirit. Or an invisible sense that someone you have loved is close by brings healing. There are so many afterlife signs.

Jana's story:

I didn't expect my mother to die, even though she got very ill and was in hospital for five months. I wasn't with her when she died, and when I heard the shocking news, I felt an urgent need to get some fresh air. I was at home and stepped outside onto my porch. Once outside, I felt my mother all around me. It was as if she was right there. I felt an invisible kiss on my cheek. I looked up and saw the wind chime my mother had given me as a house-warming present. It was a warm day and there was barely any breeze, but all of a sudden, the wind chime started to ring loud and clear. It rang without any breeze for about thirty or so seconds and then it stopped. It was a beautiful experience and meant the world to me.

Rainbows, songs, white feathers, coins, clouds or a butterfly or bird, typically a robin, crossing your path, as well as clocks stopping and lost objects being found and meaningful songs played at just the right time, rank among the most commonly reported afterlife signs. Typically, they appear during times of grief and crisis, but they can sometimes appear simply as a gentle and loving reminder that you are more than your body and your mind.

Nothing is out of bounds, as what matters is the meaningful impact on the experiencer. For example, Louise,[34] a former law lecturer from Cambridge University, believes her departed husband regularly communicates with her through a mysterious WhatsApp group. On her daughter's birthday, a WhatsApp group was formed for her, her daughter and her departed husband, but neither Louise herself nor her daughter created the group.

Kandy's[35] afterlife sign was a packet of biscuits that suddenly fell onto the floor when she was talking to her mother about her departed father and how much they all loved biscuits. Kandy believes it was her dad.

There could well be a rational explanation for all these signs, but that doesn't seem to matter. For the experiencer, it feels as if a departed loved one is beside them.

CHAOS OR PATTERN? YOU DECIDE

According to Einstein, 'There are two ways to live your life. One is as though nothing is a miracle. The other is as though everything is a miracle.'

Chaos theory argues that everything in our lives is random, but scientists are beginning to suggest that there may be patterns. It's easy to understand why – just look at the miracle design of a snow-flake or spider's web or the intricate construction of the human brain. It feels too perfect to be random, doesn't it?

I've lost count of the afterlife sign stories sent to me over the years in which 'the timing was perfect' or 'right time, right place'. Or things happening precisely when they are meant to. Yes, it could all be coincidence, but it could all be interconnected by an invisible order and purpose too. As with the afterlife, there is no definitive proof yet, so until there is, why not consider that there might just be a higher or deeper order behind coincidences, or what Jung terms 'synchronicity'. Why not believe in something that brings you greater comfort and hope?

One of the wonderful things about getting older is you can look back on your life and see all those times when you were in the right place at the right time and that even if you didn't realize it at the time, there was a pattern to it all. You also can look forward with anticipation as to what synchronicities are waiting for you.

I hope that as you have been working through your lessons you have started to become more and more aware of coincidences, associations, symbols, patterns and signs in your waking life and in your dreams.

SIGN LANGUAGE

Afterlife signs are deeply personal, and because of this they are unlikely to become a subject of scientific investigation in the way that NDEs are. However, there's no doubt they can empower your inner psychic and bring you comfort, especially if you are grieving. I want you to start giving them the same importance as your dreams. Rather like not interpreting a dream, missing a sign is like getting a personal message from your inner psychic and not reading it.

Although some are reported more often than others, be aware that literally anything[36] that fills you with a sense of awe and brings you a feeling of connection and comfort, or reminds you that you are part of something greater, or that someone you loved and lost is close by, can be regarded as a sign. The key is how it makes you *feel*.

As this lesson draws to a close, start looking at the world around you as awash with signs just waiting to be noticed by your inner psychic and medium. Your signs may be invisible at first, but stay aware and you will eventually notice them in a starry night, a shaft of sunshine, the petals of a flower, the notes of great music, in the kindness of others, or anywhere your heart takes you.

Signs and synchronicities are a beautiful blending of the external world with your inner world that can trigger a feeling of deep inner peace, a glimpse of a sparkling interconnection between everyone and everything, and a sense that you truly are a part of something greater.

Choose to read the signs. There is nothing you can do when you lose a loved one or things don't go to plan in your life, but you can choose to see a pattern and learn. You can choose to experience your life as not happening *to* you but happening *for* you, as an opportunity to experience, learn and evolve. And when you approach life with this sense of gratitude, freedom and anticipation, the mists of materialism recede and you understand that there is an unseen part of you that is eternal and separate from your body and mind. You become the soul in human form you were born to be.

WE NEED TO TALK ABOUT MEDIUMS

As you've learned, it is possible for you to become your own medium and to establish a direct connection to the afterlife, but should you ever visit a medium?[37]

There are honest mediums out there who are sincere in their desire to bring comfort and healing and who can help you adjust to the idea of connecting to loved ones in spirit.[38] But even so, I always find myself returning to my initial position of endorsing direct contact with the afterlife rather than through a medium.

One brilliant study[39] underlines my position. From 2018 to 2020, Dr Arnaud Delorme[40] from IONS conducted a study of twelve volunteer mediums and twelve volunteer controls – non-mediums. Photos were given to all twenty-four participants and they were asked to determine cause of death of a deceased person just by studying their photo. Intriguingly, the non-medium group outperformed the medium group. The mediums were nervous under lab conditions because when asked to repeat the experiment at home, their results improved. This study suggests we all have mediumistic ability and the explanation for why the control group did better in the lab was because they weren't suffering from performance anxiety and the mediums were.

I relish this study, as it shows once again that when it comes to empowering your inner psychic, expectations, forcing or straining too much can create psychic blocks. It also suggests we all have mediumistic potential and life is a better laboratory setting for the inner psychic than a research laboratory.

However, if you do feel compelled to visit a medium,[41] be sure to adhere to the suggested guidelines (*page 257*).

REGULATION

With the psychic services industry continuing to thrive, some kind of regulation is urgently required to limit the possibility of frauds and scams. Literally anyone can claim they have psychic powers and set themselves up and charge fees for services as a medium, channel, psychic, angel healer, lightworker, and so on and on.

The late sceptic James Randi famously set up a million-dollar challenge for proof of psychic ability, but although numerous psychics and mediums took up the challenge, nobody ever won. This is often held up as proof that psychic abilities aren't real, but Randi was a magician, not a scientist. I believe the world of science is the place to look for this proof. And, as you have seen in the introduction and Lesson One, visionary scientific research is starting to happen, with universities, research centres and organizations like IONS leading the way.

I am on a mission to promote scientific research into psychic and mediumship ability. I dream of a day when therapists and doctors share science of consciousness research to ease the grieving process.

Windbridge founder Dr Julie Beischel[42] gave up a lucrative career in the pharmaceutical industry following a visit to a medium who revealed with shocking accuracy the circumstances of her mother's death. This led her to wonder what would happen if mediums were tested in the same clinical way that drugs are.[43] Her research at Windbridge is a talking point, as it centres on volunteer mediums working in conditions where all possibility of fraud is removed.

In 2015 Windbridge published a study[44] involving fifty-eight readings with twenty mediums who volunteered to be tested under strict conditions to eliminate all possibility of fraud. This study is regarded as strong evidence of anomalous information by mediums – in other words, mediums receiving information from the other side without any previous knowledge of the departed or the sitters.

Wouldn't it be incredible if there were scientifically endorsed mediums, as Windbridge is currently working on with promising results, or precognitives,[45] as I tried to initiate during my collaboration with Dr Julia Mossbridge, and a free scientifically endorsed precognitive training and testing programme?

I live in hope that one day the psychic world will be embraced in this way and as well as scientifically endorsed psychics, it will be standard well-being practice for everyone to start their day with dream recall. But until that visionary day comes, remember your inner psychic – *you* – shouldn't be following anyone. During times of grief you have a remarkable opportunity to empower your inner psychic and come to the peaceful understanding that death is the beginning of a new life in spirit.

SEEING YOUR LIGHT

~~~~~~~~~~~~~~~~~~~~~~~~~~~~~~~~

Talking about death is always going to bring up intense feelings and fears, because it is the great unknown. Even if you believe in an afterlife, you may well fear death, but it is a part of life, a natural miracle like birth. Without death there can be no birth. Without endings there can be no beginnings.

When you die, you leave your body behind and become pure consciousness. I don't know what dying is like because I haven't been on that great adventure yet. I have had many reports from people who have had an NDE or an afterlife vision and met departed loved ones and angels on the other side. They tell me that the afterlife is a place of light and continuous learning.

As for the dying process itself, from what my research has uncovered, initially people have no awareness that they have died. They float over their body and look down on it. Then, when realization comes, the material world turns to mist. They feel liberated and free. At this moment, a feeling of intense unconditional love sweeps them away to another level of existence, where learning and evolving into higher and higher versions of themselves remain the theme. Many say that human words fail to capture the essence of what they have experienced. A few have told me that a 1998 movie starring the late Robin Williams entitled *What Dreams May Come* comes close to depicting some of the infinite possibility of the other side. The idea that death is but a dream[46] is in line with those ancient beliefs that the dream state is a portal to the afterlife.

The afterlife differs from account to account and is often deeply personal, suggesting that every day we are creating, with our thoughts, feelings and actions, the kind of afterlife we will experience.

What a life-changing thought!

CROSSING YOUR OWN SEA OF STARS

In 2022 NASA's James Webb telescope released breathtaking images[47] of stars and galaxies. Do check them out, as they are widely available online.

In the preface, I referenced the astronaut Edgar Mitchell and his transcendent experience when heading back to Earth. But you can experience this sense of transcendence every day without becoming an astronaut. It's impossible to star gaze or look at images from outer space without feeling a deep inner sense of interconnection, awe and eternity.

Stars are made of the same energy as you are. Perhaps those you have loved and lost are like the stars watching over you. Perhaps you will join them when it is your time to leave behind the material and cross over.

I hope this lesson has helped you see death, if not as a miracle, at least in a new psychic light, and opened you up to the idea that your consciousness never dies and you can connect to immortality in any moment.

Think of it this way: the 'child you' and 'yesterday you' have 'died', but your consciousness carries on in the consciousness of the person you are today. It is perhaps your consciousness that lives on when you die.

You are a psychic being having a human experience.

REINVENTING YOUR WHEEL

Congratulations. Give yourself a standing ovation.

You have completed Lesson Seven of seven, but please don't rest on your laurels. Be sure to read the conclusion mindfully now, as it contains a few important insights to help you on your way. There is a little more illumination in the resources section too.

Then you might just want to reinvent your wheel – or should I say your spiral – and start right at the beginning of this book again. Psychic growth is like a spiral, where each time you end up where you started, you have, without realizing it at the time, moved forward, and you see the same things from a higher or deeper perspective.

So, with each and every reading may your inner psychic grow clearer, stronger, higher and wiser and take you ever onwards in the direction of your dreams and ever higher and higher to your own infinite stars.

PART THREE

Conclusion

'It is you. The whole theory of the universe is directed unerringly to one single individual – namely you.'
Walt Whitman

CONCLUSION

You Again

When you open up to the idea of yourself as an eternal being living in an eternal now, nothing feels the same again. You understand what your inner psychic has always known – that life is a process of endless becoming. The secret to happiness is just to fully experience and relish the process.

Nothing illustrates this ultimate life hack better than a sublime movie I urge you all to watch as homework to complement your entire inner psychic empowerment programme. It's the Disney animated Oscar-winning movie *Soul*. I have collaborated with members of the science team[1] who helped craft, with sensitivity, and as much accuracy as possible from NDE accounts, the afterlife scenes in this movie.

During the movie, the lead character, Joe, achieves his musical ambitions, but notices that it doesn't feel as good as he thought. Dorothea, his muse, tells him the tale of a little fish who swims up to an older fish and asks how to find 'this thing called the ocean'. The older fish tells the young one that they are both in the ocean right now. The younger fish struggles to process this, as all he sees and knows is water, saying that what he wants is the ocean.

Joe believes his happiness is connected to his dream of becoming a musician. But when he gets to live his dream, he is disappointed that he doesn't feel that different. He's the same person!

Many of us fail to realize, just as Joe initially does, that living a meaningful life isn't about expressing our talents, or achieving fame, popularity and wealth, or even finding purpose through accomplishing our goals or living our dreams. It is about finding joy in everyday things and just winging it in every moment. I will never tire of saying this: it is about the experience, not about the destination.

Even if your life doesn't go as planned, or your big dreams don't come true, or you mess up, you can still live a deeply meaningful life if you are adaptable, learn to appreciate what you have, and live authentically and with passion in the present. Indeed, a sure-fire sign of living an empowered life is course-correcting a lot, because you aren't afraid to experiment, learn and discover.

SETBACKS HAPPEN

Setbacks happen for a reason. They are a big opportunity to learn, evolve, find inner courage, and also to be extra kind to yourself. Never beat yourself up when you are down. Help yourself stand up again. Remember you are the person, the love of your life, that you have been looking for.

Your inner psychic empowerment rituals are all designed to help you help yourself. They are sacred self-care acts that you can do every day from now on to show yourself and the universe that you know who you truly are – a psychic being with supernormal abilities, such as intuition, empathy[2] and kindness, that you can activate at any time. Studies[3] have shown that these innate sensitive[4] traits hold the keys to a meaningful life.

Your inner psychic is always pointing you towards self-awareness and finding meaning in the present moment, in the actual experience of living. And finding that meaning not on the horizon or when you have jumped through assorted hoops, but in the here and now.

You can start finding that meaning right now. Read between the lines. Smile. Make the most of this moment. You only get to live it once.

S – see
M – mystery/magic
I – in
L – life
E – every day

And always, always remember the four essential Ls: Live, Learn, Love, LAUGH.

EVERYDAY EMPOWERMENT

Now *use* your psychic abilities in all the areas of your life.

YOUR RELATIONSHIPS

Use your psychic abilities to help you sense the people who will lift you up and let go of those who will drag you down. Allow the observational approach this book has championed to help you read people better. Notice what is beneath the surface in all your interactions. Listen and reflect more and speak and judge less.

Use inner psychic manifesting techniques to send out positive vibes to someone you want to get closer to or attract into your life.

Simply think about them with feelings of love and joy. If the attraction is meant to be, it will happen, but if it doesn't, trust that someone more suited to you is out there. It's just a matter of time before you meet them.

Bear in mind, though, that when it comes to relationships, the one relationship your inner psychic is most obsessed with is the relationship you have with yourself. This is because others tend to treat you not as you treat them, but as you treat yourself. You can't love others if you don't love yourself. You need to become your own best friend. (This isn't selfish and it isn't narcissism – as narcissists[5] have zero empathy – and if you ever encounter someone who love bombs and confuses you or plays mind games with you, block them from your life.)

Choosing to love and respect yourself each day may take time, especially if your childhood wasn't easy and self-criticism has become engrained. But you can do it. Your inner psychic can help you get there. Simple things like marking a tick or a heart on a wall calendar for each day you show up for yourself can really help. Or you could allow the unconditional love of a pet to help you appreciate just how amazing you are. But simply knowing that feelings of gratitude and love can somehow create a happiness-attracting forcefield, and that feelings inspire brain- and life-changing thoughts and beliefs, should be all the inspiration you need to love yourself as if your life depended on it.

In time, you may find that your loving and positive relationship with yourself is enough to sustain you, or you may find that you naturally attract like-minded souls. Being single or in a relationship – neither life choice is superior. The only thing that matters is whether your relationships with yourself and with others bring you joy. And if you have ever had your heart broken, rather like bereavement, your inner psychic can help you see this as an opportunity for significant personal growth, as the way forward is to find within yourself the love you gave away. Your heart isn't actually broken. It is in training,[6] because, like a muscle, the more you use it, the stronger and wiser it gets.

Your inner psychic will help you release people who don't have your best interests at heart, but if you do encounter difficult people, a helpful psychic tip is to see the inner child or vulnerable disconnected part of them. You never know what others are going through behind the scenes, so a rule of thumb is to always be kind. So often when people are cruel or vindictive it is because deep down they feel alone and scared and have no connection to their own power.

And when your inner psychic is empowered, you no longer take what others say or do personally (because it's always about them and not you), and you let go of any expectations of how you want others to behave. The biggest mistake people make in relationships is falling in love with the potential of someone or what they could be, rather than the reality. You can't change someone so they make you happy. The only person you can change is yourself. Feel joyful about being yourself and the rest just flows.

YOUR HEALTH

There is a connection between a healthy mind and a healthy body, as we saw earlier (*page 173*). I'm not going to suggest that your inner psychic is a miracle healer – it isn't – but what it can do is encourage you to send loving thoughts to every cell in your body. And this loving intention will motivate you to treat your body with deep respect, as the temple of your soul, by having a nutritious diet, exercising regularly, getting plenty of fresh air and quality sleep, and avoiding toxic substances.

YOUR WORK

Your inner psychic will always aim to help you see that in every aspect of your life, including your career, you are in control. You do have choice. Yes, you may have to work hard to pay the bills, but you choose how you react to your job, your work, your life.

If you aren't sure what you should be doing, experiment! These days the 'career for life' mantra is fast disappearing and you may retrain and/or switch jobs many times. That's okay, because every life path is an opportunity to learn and grow.

And don't make the mistake (as Joe did in *Soul*) of confusing your work with your purpose. Your inner psychic is always more concerned about your self-development than any work that you do, however inspired. It is a cliché but, like many clichés, so true – and hospice workers[7] would agree – that nobody on their deathbed[8] says, 'I wish I had spent more time at the office.' Indeed, in their final days, people rarely regret what they did. They regret what they didn't do!

Leaving this Earth without regrets is what your inner psychic has in store for you.

YOUR WEALTH

If money, status, talent, good looks, popularity and a great career are the secret to happiness, why do so many wealthy, successful, beautiful people struggle with depression or addiction and in some cases take their own lives?

Money won't make you happy if your relationship with yourself is toxic. If more of us valued what truly matters in life, it would be a happier world. That's why your inner psychic isn't that bothered about making you rich, or super popular. That may well come in time, as money can be used for tremendous good, but only when you have done the inner work. If that's in place then you're wealthy already.

YOUR BIG AND SMALL STUFF

Empowering your inner psychic can also help you with more every-day things like sensing where to park the car or finding something you've lost or deciding whether to call someone or not. It can also alert you to potential threats or dangers and bring you a sense of comfort and hope when you feel alone.

Whenever you ask for help, your inner psychic will speak to you through your clear psychic senses and through everyday signs. Your inner psychic will also bring to your notice books, people, events or ideas that will guide, heal and inspire you. You will have a sense that there is a pattern at work in your life and nothing is ever triv-ial. Even the smallest thing can change the course of your future. Coincidences can carry great weight. Something as inconsequential as missing a train, like in the movie *Sliding Doors*, can mean that you meet or experience something life-changing.

Of course it can't be proven, but what if it is true that everything happens for a reason, and every moment, however seemingly unimportant or trivial at the time, might potentially change your life? This is a high-vibration way to live. It focuses your attention on the meaning and potential of the present to create a better future. Being fully engaged in the potential of now is exactly where your inner psychic wants you to be.

YOUR PURPOSE

It is my sincere hope that from this moment on you will never lack meaning or purpose again.

You will know that a better life starts *now*, with the next positive or courageous thing you choose to think, recall, feel, do, imagine and dream. With the next thing you learn about yourself.

Every time you learn from your mistakes, are kind to yourself, speak with authenticity, act with integrity and humility and feel grateful and do your best you are on your way to becoming the empowered psychic you were born to be. And when you switch your inner light on, it inspires others to seek their own inner peace and joy, setting off a ripple effect. When others follow your example, a quantum evolutionary leap into a more united, compassionate and loving world is no longer an impossible dream.

So, a better world really can start whenever you decide to empower your inner psychic. It starts with one single person – you.

Many of us hope to change the world for the better, but don't realize that the only way we can begin to do that is by *first* changing and empowering ourselves. Remember everyone has an innate psychic sense, even if they aren't aware of it yet. If you are helping others without also taking care of your own needs, any help you give will be draining to them on an invisible energetic level rather than vitalizing.

YOUR INNER PSYCHIC BLUEPRINT

~~~~~~~~~~~~~~~~~~~~~~~~~~~~~~

There's no one-size-fits-all blueprint for becoming your own psychic, but you can't go wrong with the following three steps:

- ☾ **DAILY MEDITATION:** Just a few minutes of meditation each day nourishes the intuitive and creative parts of your brain.
- ☾ **GO GREEN:** Natural surroundings are your daily soul food.
- ☾ **LIVE SACRED:** Performing daily rituals, like those recommended in this book, awakens and empowers your innate psychic senses.

There's no doubt you have psychic abilities. The only doubt is whether you are going to use them now as a source of personal guidance. Are they going to remain dormant or are you going to unleash them?

I can't tell you what is best for you to do. You always have a choice. You always have free will. What I can suggest, though, is to do what makes you feel good. If you are feeling joyful then there's every indication you are heading in the right direction, and whether you realize it or not, you are in tune with and empowering your inner psychic. If, however, you feel anxious, then your current path isn't optimum for your highest good. Time for a new direction.

NO GOING BACK NOW

When you move past your thoughts and don't allow what is happening around you to define you, you arrive at your inner psychic, the real you. Your inner psychic speaks in your voice. It sees the world with your eyes. It hears with your ears, feels with your heart and knows with your mind. It's all about *you.*

Once your inner psychic is active, you'll have all the guidance you need to help you cope and find meaning, whatever life throws at you. You'll know that it is fine to change direction, take another path if you feel guided to do so. You'll also know that there's no going back to how your life was before.

Nothing will ever feel the same again, because from now on you'll see beyond the material and understand that the best things in life are unseen and infinite. You won't feel alone because you'll know you are interconnected with the energy of everyone and everything.

This is enlightenment. Joy. Bliss. Flow. Peak experience. Empowerment. You are that drop in an ocean, that ocean in a drop, and your energy originates from and connects you to universal consciousness.

You see yourself in others. There is no separation, and just like symbols from a dream, everything and everyone you encounter in your waking life becomes an opportunity to learn, help, heal and evolve. You have deep compassion for others, as their pain is your pain and their joy your joy. Your instinct is to care about both yourself and others.

The more you go within, the more any sense of separateness from the universe vanishes. Not only does it become abundantly clear to you that the universe is on your side, you also know clearly that you can count on yourself in every moment.

You are your own dream decoder, oracle, psychic, medium, guide, angel, shaman and guru. The Earth is your school[9] and the infinite potential to evolve into higher and higher versions of yourself is your birthright. From now on you are an unstoppable and unlimited charismatic force because, whether facing triumph or disaster, you have your own back. You are forever becoming the person of your dreams!

FREEDOM

Your inner psychic is the voice of your soul, your authentic self,[10] urging you to have courage and to trust yourself, because when you do that, you are liberated. Like wild horses running along a beach, you are *free*.

This book has given you the knowledge and the tools. It's time now for you to make the best use of them by liberating your inner psychic not just now and again, but always. Your life isn't changed by the occasional, it is changed by the repeated – what you repeatedly believe, sense and do. So repeatedly trust your inner guide and make your psychic empowerment rituals your everyday.

Once you trust yourself and realize you have access to your own psychic power, the doors to the universe will be flung wide open for you, and you have within you all you need to astonish yourself and others with newfound possibilities every single day.

You learn in the classroom outside your comfort zone. So get out there and fail and fail again. You won't be perfect, and your life won't be perfect either, because perfection is boring and it doesn't teach you anything. But you will be a truly beautiful example of someone who knows how to learn, love, laugh and live life as it was meant to be lived – deeply, freely, passionately!

I shall leave you, for now, with two of my favourite quotes to reflect on. May they be a source of endless illumination for you in dark places, when all the other lights go out ...

*'The best things in life are unseen.
That's why we close our eyes when
we kiss, cry and dream.'*

Helen Keller

'Not all who wander are lost.'

The Lord of the Rings

Resources

Get in Touch

If you have a question, story or insight, please don't hesitate to get in touch with me.

☾ You can email me at: angeltalk710@aol.com. You can also message me via www.theresacheung.com or my author pages on Facebook and Twitter and my Instagram handle @thetheresacheung. I aim to reply to everyone in due course.

☾ You can also listen to my *White Shores* podcast – the podcast for psychic beings. *White Shores* is available on all podcast platforms and features interviews with some of the world's leading scientists researching consciousness and the paranormal, as well as true-life stories, expert insight, rituals, dream interpretation, psychic development, laughter, music and more.

Free gift

And anyone who gets in touch with me listing at least five of the *Lord of the Rings* quotes in this book – both those directly quoted and, even better, the ones that are subtly hidden in the text – will receive a *free Empower your Inner Psychic* gift.

Organizations

The Academy for the Advancement of Postmaterialist Sciences

www.aapsglobal.com

Promotes open-minded evidence-based enquiry into postmaterialist consciousness research.

The Arthur Findlay College

www.authurfindlaycollege.org

This psychic training college offers advice, courses, talks, information and training for potential mediums.

The Association for the Scientific Study of Anomalous Phenomena

www.assap.ac.uk

Charity and learned society founded in 1981 to investigate, research and educate on a wide range of anomalous phenomena. Also carries out paranormal investigations and trains members to become accredited investigators.

The Association for Spiritual Integrity (ASI)

https://www.spiritual-integrity.org/
(*White Shores*, Season 6, Episode 38)

The mission of the Association for Spiritual Integrity™ is to foster the fundamental role of strong ethical principles in the ongoing development of spiritual leaders and communities. The ASI is a voluntary, inclusive, international organization of spiritual leaders, teachers and guides.

Buddha at the Gas Pump BATGAP

https://batgap.com/

YouTube channel hosted by Rick Archer (*White Shores*, Season 6, Ep. 1) with free videos with ordinary people and spiritual thought leaders who have experienced awakenings.

The Centre for the Study of Anomalous Psychological Processes, University of Northampton

https://www.northampton.ac.uk/

Conducts research in the areas of parapsychological and transpersonal psychology.

The College of Psychic Studies

www.collegeofpsychicstudies.co.uk

An educational charity offering regular classes, workshops, lectures and consultations in the field of psychic development.

Psychic Science – ESP Cards

www.psychicscience.org/esp2

The targets used for these tests are the standard ESP cards (sometimes called Zener cards) as used by the parapsychologist J.B. Rhine in his classic studies of extrasensory perception. These show five different symbols and you can use them here to test yourself.

Three organizations for the bereaved:

The Forever Family Foundation

www.foreverfamilyfoundation.org

Furthers the understanding of afterlife science through research and education, while providing support and healing for people in grief.

Helping Parents Heal

www.helpingparentsheal.org

Non-profit spiritual organization dedicated to assisting bereaved parents.

The Shared Crossing Project

www.sharedcrossing.com

Organization dedicated to raising awareness about end-of-life experiences.

The Galileo Commission

www.galileocommission.org

The Galileo Commission's remit is to open public discourse and to find ways to expand science so that it can accommodate and explore important human experiences and questions that science, in its present form, is unable to integrate.

The Institute of HeartMath

www.heartmath.org

Provides free education and training programmes, services, research membership and tools and technology to transform people's lives by deepening their connection with their own hearts and the hearts of others for a peaceful future.

The Institute of Love and Time (TILT)

https://loveandtime.org

Committed to providing evidence-based non-addictive humane technologies that allow people to have a deeper and more loving connection with themselves over time, and from that place to create a happier and healthier future.

The Institute of Noetic Sciences (IONS)

www.noetic.org

Science-based non-profit research, education and membership organization dedicated to consciousness research and educational outreach, engaging a global learning community in the realization of human potential.

Noetic.org/theresa-cheung/

This link takes you to a page specially created by IONS for Theresa Cheung readers. There are three wonderful *free gifts* from their research library waiting for you to download there.

The Koestler Parapsychology Unit (KPU)

www.koestler-parapsychology.psy.ed.ac.uk

Research group based in the Psychology Department of the University of Edinburgh. Established in 1985, it consists of academics who teach and research various aspects of parapsychology.

The Parapsychological Association

www.parapsych.org

International professional organization of scientists and scholars engaged in the scientific study of psychic experiences.

The Premonition Code

www.thepremonitioncode.com

Website dedicated to *The Premonition Code* by neuroscientist Dr Julia Mossbridge and myself, where you can access free online lectures and scientifically endorsed precognition training.

The Rhine Research Center

www.rhine.org

Advances the science of parapsychology, provides education and resources for the public and fosters a community for individuals with personal and professional interest in *psi*.

The Shift Network

http://theshiftnetwork.com

Founded by Stephen Dinan (*White Shores* guest, Season 6, Ep. 36) the Shift Network offers a wealth of both free and paid-for programmes to assist people in navigating their personal healing journeys. You may want to check out their Dreamwork 2022 summit, which I had the honour to co-host.

The Society for Psychical Research

www.spr.ac.uk

Founded in 1882 to conduct scholarly research into human experiences that challenge contemporary scientific models.

The Society for Scientific Exploration

www.scientificexploration.org

A forum for sharing research into conventional and unconventional topics that cross mainstream boundaries and have profound implications for human knowledge and technology.

Time Machine

www.timemachine.love

Record time travel narratives to your past and future selves.

The Windbridge Research Institute

www.windbridge.org

Independent research organization consisting of scientists and specialists researching mediumship and the paranormal. If you wish to book online readings with reasonably priced, scientifically endorsed and ethical mediums, this is the place to visit.

Suggested Reading

Alexander, Eben and Newell, Karen, *Living in a Mindful Universe* (Piatkus, 2017).

Auerbach, Loyd, *Psychic Dreams* (Llewellyn, 2017).

Barušs, Imants and Mossbridge, Julia, *Transcendent Mind: Rethinking the science of consciousness* (American Psychological Association, 2016).

Carter, Chris, *Science and the Near-Death Experience: How consciousness survives death* (Inner Traditions International, 2010).

Cheung, Theresa, *The Dream Dictionary A to Z* (HarperCollins, 2019).

—, *The Dream Decoder Pack and Journal* (Laurence King, 2019).

—, *The Sensitive Soul* (Thread, Bookouture, 2019).

—, *How to Catch a Dream* (Harper Thorsons, 2022).

—, and Mossbridge, Julia, *The Premonition Code* (Watkins, 2017).

Coelho, Paulo, *The Alchemist* (HarperCollins, 1995).

Cooper, Callum, *Telephone Calls from the Dead* (www.callumecooper.com).

Dossey, Larry, *One Mind: How our individual mind is part of a greater consciousness and why it matters* (Hay House, 2014).

Emoto, Masaru, *The Hidden Messages in Water* (Simon & Schuster, 2011).

Frankl, Viktor, *Man's Search for Meaning* (Verlag für Jugend und Volk, 1946; Rider, 2004).

Freke, Timothy, *Soul Story: Evolution and the purpose of life* (Watkins, 2017).

Gladwell, Malcolm, *Blink* (Penguin, 2006).

Johnson, Clare, *The Art of Transforming Nightmares* (Llewellyn, 2021).

Kean, Leslie, *Surviving Death: A journalist investigates evidence for an afterlife* (Three Rivers, 2018).

Kübler-Ross, Elisabeth, *On Grief and Grieving* (Simon & Schuster, 2014).

Lachman, Gary, *Dreaming Ahead of Time* (Floris, 2022).

Lowenberg, Lauri, *Dream on It* (Saint Martin's, 2011).

Mackesy, Charlie, *The Boy, the Mole, the Fox and the Horse* (Ebury, 2019).

Moody, Raymond, *Life After Life* (Mockingbird Books, 1975; HarperCollins, 2015).

—, *Coming Back* (Create Space, 2017).

Radin, Dean, *Supernormal* (Chopra Press, 2013).

—, *Real Magic* (Penguin, 2018).

Redfield, James, *The Celestine Prophecy* (Bantam, 1994).

Ruiz, Don Miguel, *The Four Agreements* (Amber Allen, 2018).

Schwartz, Gary E. and Simon, William L., *The Afterlife Experiments* (Simon & Schuster Australia, 2002).

Sheldrake, Rupert, *The Sense of Being Stared at and Other Aspects of the Extended Mind* (Cornerstone, 2013).

Smith, Carlyle, *Heads Up Dreaming* (Turnstone Press, 2014).

Targ, Russell, *The Reality of ESP: A physicist's proof of psychic abilities* (Quest, 2012).

Tolle, Eckhart, *The Power of Now* (Yellow Kite, 2001).

Wahbeh, Helané: *The Science of Channelling* (New Harbinger, 2021).

Wargo, Eric, *Time Loops* (Anomalist, 2018).

Inner Psychic Tools A to Z

The list below is by necessity brief and there are bound to be omissions. You may agree or you may not agree with the perspective I offer on each system, and that is perfectly fine. But if you agree or disagree strongly, please consider why. If you were collating this A to Z list, what psychic notes would you make and why? What would you include that I haven't mentioned here? The aim of this list is not to get you to agree with me, but to give you pause for thought, so if you want to use psychic tools in your inner psychic empowerment programme, you can make your own mind up.

ALCHEMY

Centuries ago this was the term used for transforming everyday metal into gold, but in the personal and spiritual growth industry, it refers to working towards your highest or purest self.

The alchemical transformation process may involve the use of crystals, spells, rituals, herbs and potions that harness the energy of natural elements to help bring about meaningful change in a person's life. Indeed, alchemy[1] is sometimes considered a higher form of magic. It is typically shrouded in mystery by alchemists, which can make it seem unnecessarily complicated and impenetrable to the outsider. At the end of the day, it is simply a spiritual philosophy that can be used to help you understand and connect to your own inner transformative power. In other words, the best alchemist to visit is already within you. It's your inner psychic!

ANCESTRAL HEALING

This is the process of discovering and releasing trauma that you may have inherited from your ancestors. There is scientific backing for intergenerational trauma, and if you have ever researched your family tree, you may find a number of themes that seem to pass through the bloodlines from one generation to the next. The aim of ancestral healing is to ensure that you break a negative cycle.

Reflecting on your family tree and understanding what inherited cultural and family trauma you may unconsciously be carrying with you is something you can research and reflect on yourself. The same applies to ancestral healing techniques, such as journaling, thought shifting, and meditation to help you reprogramme and remove inherited irrational fears.

ANGEL HEALING

Angels are typically associated with religion, but in recent years they have formed a spiritual movement of their own, independent of it. They are said to be pure spiritual beings[2] that can connect you to the forces for goodness within and around you. Some psychics claim to be able to see angels complete with traditional wings and halo. Others communicate with them psychically, or claim to have extensive knowledge of them and offer angel healing readings and courses.[3]

Angel healing is based around angel hierarchies and involves a lightworker invoking the healing vibration of a specific angel to release roadblocks to your spiritual growth.

Whether or not a lightworker can see or invoke the healing power of angels – or even whether angels are real in the first place – is immaterial here. The important thing is what can *you* see and sense. If you are drawn to angels – and don't be surprised if you are, as who doesn't want to think there are loving angels watching over them? – do understand that what you are actually drawn to is the energetic potential for goodness, compassion, love and light within and around you. In essence, your inner psychic!

Archangel healing

I'm not entirely sure why angel healing isn't enough and archangels are elevated above them, or even why there are female and male archangels. It is a very human way of thinking about angels, rather like a spiritual LinkedIn, but we are human beings, so it makes sense. One way to look at all this breaking down of angel energy into categories and hierarchies is that it can help you understand the expansive holistic nature of loving energies within and around you better. To risk repeating myself, your inner psychic!

ASTROLOGY

This is the ancient art of charting the positions of the planets and stars when you were born in the 12 signs of the zodiac that the heavens are divided into. Each zodiac sign has archetypal, or universally applicable, characteristics and potentials.

The 'as above, so below' concept has scientific evidence to support it. (The moon rules the tides for example, and humans are up to 70 per cent water.) Astrology[4] is an absorbing psychological self-help tool that can help you understand yourself and others better. It can also be used to predict future trends in your life by looking at the forward movement of the planets and comparing planetary patterns from the past with current situations. However, as with any predictive tool, this can only point to a potential future, given you always have free will.

Most of us are familiar with the characteristics of our sun sign – the position of the sun when we were born – but for more in-depth analysis, your entire birthchart, with the position of all the planets, needs to be drawn up.[5] A professional astrologer can do this for you and help you interpret it, but there are many free online resources which can do it for you as well. All you need to enter is the time, date and location of your birth.

As long as you know your sun (ego), moon (emotions), Saturn (teacher) and rising (how others see you) sign, you truly have more than enough psychological self-help material to work with. More in-depth or detailed astrology than that carries with it the serious risk of falling into a rabbit-hole of jargon and endless speculation.

AUTOMATIC WRITING

This is a very pure way to connect to your inner psychic, but it might need a lot of time and practice. The idea is that you mull over a problem you have or something you need insight on and then you simply write or draw on a blank piece of paper the first thing that comes to your mind, however nonsensical. When you do this for the first time, limit yourself to five minutes. Don't be surprised if nothing comes through on your first attempt. You need to give this channelling (*see page 172*) technique time. If you have ever doodled without thinking, this is the relaxed but creative response you are aiming for here.

And if you are thinking, or are told, that the writing comes from so-called spirits moving the pen, that isn't the case. In my humble opinion, any wisdom that comes through is entirely from the person doing the writing.

BIBLIOMANCY

This is one of my favourite psychic empowerment tools because it's so easy. You just need a book with plenty of pages of text that you feel connected to (I'd love it if you used this one).

Sit somewhere quiet, close your eyes, hold the book and ask it to tell you something you need to know. Then open it at a random page. Keep your eyes closed and put your finger on the page. Then open your eyes and read where your finger took you. Allow your inner psychic to interpret those words, using what you have learned in Lesson Four about the power of symbol and metaphor.

CRYSTAL HEALING

Watch the Disney movie *Dumbo* about an elephant with huge ears. He is given a white feather and told that if he holds it with his trunk he can fly, but he has to learn that he could fly all along. The white feather just helped him believe it.

I believe that crystals work in the same way. Although they may emit certain vibrations, there isn't any solid proof yet they can heal or enhance your psychic power. But if you believe they work, they will.

As an aside, I love and use crystals. Sometimes we all need a good luck charm or an inspiring companion on our journey through life. There's no harm in carrying one around with you to boost your psychic self-confidence or placing one in your bedroom to boost your dream recall or to help you meditate or manifest or do readings for yourself.

I recommend rose quartz for self-love, clear quartz and moonstone for vivid dream recall, amethyst and lapis lazuli for boosting intuition, but there is a whole world of beautiful psychic friendly crystals out there just waiting for you to discover, wear and love. Do your research on their properties, but at the end of the day let a crystal call your name.

Note: You may also want to research essential oils, as like crystals, there is some research to suggest they can be beneficial, although the majority of evidence is anecdotal. You need to find what essential oil feels right for you, but for inner psychic work you can't go wrong with my favourites, rose oil, clary sage, frankincense and sandalwood.

I CHING

The I Ching[6] or 'Book of Changes' is an ancient Chinese divination manual which interprets a series of hexagrams (symbols made up of six lines) formed by tossing coins or sticks to give answers to questions. There are sixty-four hexagrams and each represents a process in nature or human nature.

In many respects, the I Ching is a study of how life changes over time. The theory is that understanding the patterns and cycles of change can help you make the right decisions and prepare you for the future. It has been used in China for over 5,000 years.

You are unlikely to find many professional *I Ching* readers, as experts believe the most effective way to use the system is to use it yourself. It can appear daunting at first, but as with every divination system, the more you research it and start using it, the easier and more natural it feels.

The life wisdom offered for each hexagram is profound, as it is based on shared human experiences, and for that reason the *I Ching* can be a source of ongoing illumination.

NUMEROLOGY

This is the theory, dating back to ancient times and the Greek philosopher Pythagoras, that everything carries with it the energy of or can be broken down into a number, and those numbers have certain associations and meanings. Understanding the associations of the numbers[7] in your life, from the day you were born to your house number, can help you understand yourself and the world around you better. Numbers can also be helpful signs along the way.

Numerology[8] may sound complicated, but it is actually really simple to master once you understand that all the significant numbers in your life are downsized to a single digit. For example, if you were born on 9 July, you add seven (month) and nine (day), which makes sixteen, and then you add one and six, which makes your 'birthday personality potential' the number seven. Just keep adding the numbers until you get a single digit. And once you have researched the meanings of the numbers one to nine, you can then incorporate the power of number wisdom into your life.

'Master numbers' are when numbers repeat, in particular eleven and twenty-two, and they are considered especially significant. Don't be surprised if after reading this you start to notice 11.11 more on watches or texts or emails. This is often regarded as a sign that an angel is watching over you.

Warning: Noticing number signs in your life can become addictive!

PALM-READING

Palm-reading, or palmistry, dates back to ancient China, India and Rome, and may well be one of the oldest divination systems that is still in common use today. (As an aside, when I was doing research for my HarperCollins *Element Encyclopedia of the Psychic World*, I uncovered countless ancient divination systems that have fallen out of popular use, from alomancy – divination by random patterns of salt – to zoomancy – divination by the behaviour of animals.)

A palmist will simply look at the lines on your hand to divine your future. There are lines that relate to life, fate, relationships, money, etc.

Face-reading is very similar to palmistry. You can learn both yourself online or through books and courses.

Your body is influenced by your genetics and by what you do, think and feel, and a person's hands and face can reveal much of substance about them, but, as with all methods of divination, the art is in the interpretation.

And a line on your hand cannot create your future. Only you can do that.

PAST-LIFE HEALING

The idea that your soul has had past lives and will have future lives is compelling and it does help explain why bad things happen to good people. Therapy to uncover past-life (and future-life) memories is believed to be healing.[9] There's some research on reincarnation (*see page 46*), but as intoxicating as it can be to get caught up in past or future-life dramas, when it comes to your inner psychic, remember that your power is always in the you that you are right now. And there's more than enough for you to be understanding, healing and dealing with in your current life without letting past or future-life adventures distract you.

PENDULUM DOWSING

This can be used for instant answers to problems or questions you may have. It's quite simple: as you hold the pendulum, it will rotate one way for 'yes' and the other for 'no'. Or it may move from side to side. Experiment to see how it communicates with you.

A well-known way to use it is to hold it over a pregnant woman's bump to predict the gender of the baby. You ask, 'Is it a girl?' When I was pregnant with my son, a fortune-teller used a pendulum to tell me I was going to have a girl, and when I *was* pregnant with a girl, another pendulum attempt from a psychic correctly predicted a girl. Perhaps the problem here was that I needed to hold the pendulum myself or, better still, simply trust my gut feeling about the sex of my unborn child, which was right on both occasions.

Pendulums are great fun to experiment with, but they do carry the risk of you unconsciously affecting the movement of the pendulum with tiny muscle reactions, which is known as the ideometer effect. It's also for this reason that Ouija[10] or talking boards or dowsing rods might not be ideal for you to use until you feel confident this won't be the case.

PSYCHEDELICS

The ingestion of certain psychedelics to induce psychic experiences has research[11] behind it. However, taking drugs is not advised, for the simple reason that it diminishes you. It suggests that something external or extra is needed. You don't need a mushroom to become 'psychic'; you are already psychic. You don't need psychedelics. You need self-belief.

REIKI

See 'Energy Healing' (*page 175*).

RUNES

These are alphabet letters used in ancient times by Scandinavians. The letters were originally inscribed on stones known as runestones. Each runestone has a symbol and each symbol has a meaning.

A runestone reading[12] can offer insight into problems or predict potential futures in much the same way as a Tarot card reading (*see below*). In recent years, runes have enjoyed newfound popularity due to their use in movie franchises such as *Harry Potter* and *Game of Thrones*.

SCRYING

This is the term perhaps most associated with fortune-telling. It involves looking at a reflective surface, such as a crystal ball, mirror, bowl of water or even a flame or your thumbnail, and thinking of a question. The visual shapes and symbols can offer guidance or reveal the future. Tea-leaf reading works in the same way. A fortune-teller will read the shapes left by the leaves in an empty tea cup. In other words, it's clear seeing, and you don't need to visit a fortune-teller to activate that visual psychic potential within you.

TAROT CARDS

These ancient illustrated cards date right back to medieval times, perhaps originating in Italy, and they have continued to thrive ever since. They are often thought to have occult or magical powers that can only be interpreted by a professional reader, but they don't have magical powers and they are easy for you to learn to read yourself.

Every card in the pack has an archetypal meaning based on the number, character or scene depicted by the card, and in a Tarot[13] reading they are laid out in a pattern which gives indications about your past, present and future. The traditional meanings of the cards can be easily researched online, although I highly recommend Rachel Pollack's classic Tarot book: *78 Degrees of Wisdom* (Thorsons, 1998). Then it is up to you to see what personal associations are triggered.

A Tarot or oracle card reader can offer you their perspective on what they feel a reading means for you, but – and I'm aware this is getting repetitive now, but there is power in repetition – your inner psychic only really pays attention when you are the one doing the interpreting.

Advice for Visiting Mediums and Psychics

The advice here is primarily for mediums, but applies to psychics, lightworkers, channels, energy healers, or anyone who claims they can receive information from the unseen realms and connect to unseen forces on your behalf.

I certainly don't recommend you visit a medium in the first year of your loss, as your emotions will be too raw. You need to adjust to the loss of that physical presence. Also, your departed loved one needs to adjust to their new life in spirit. It's a shock for them too. Never visit a medium or psychic when you feel vulnerable.

When you do feel ready, it's always best to choose a certified medium. To become a Windbridge certified medium requires several years of scientific testing. Few qualify, but those who do are listed on the centre's website (*see page 242*).

If a medium isn't certified, look at their training. There are many mediumship training programmes run by respected establishments like the Arthur Findlay College in the UK. If the medium's background is obscure or celebrity endorsed, steer clear. Be especially wary if they have a cult-like following.

At the end of the day, trust your inner psychic. Some untrained but sincere mediums work authentically without charging anything at local Spiritualist churches and psychic fairs. Experiment by all means, but keep your sceptical hat on.

Avoid if:

- ☉ They charge huge fees. Reasonable fees are understandable, as you are paying for someone's time and expertise, but I don't advise paying more than the price of a good haircut.
- ☉ There is excessive marketing or social media endorsement, or a book or expensive course being promoted. This is about creating a spiritual celebrity, not about empowering a client.
- ☉ They encourage repeat visits – no more than one or two visits in total are advised.
- ☉ They don't have a code of ethics.
- ☉ They tell you what to do. The only person qualified to know what is best for you is you. If you feel uncertain and in need of support, go to a qualified counsellor, not a medium or psychic.
- ☉ They are overly serious and make you feel inferior in any way. If a medium is in contact with spirit, there will be a joyful and positive energy about them. The message they give you should be empowering and make you feel confident about yourself and your ability to make your own decisions.
- ☉ They insist on in-person readings. The most convincing research on mediums so far at Windbridge was done via the phone to remove any chance of cold reading (reading the body language and other unconscious clues of the sitter), but having said that, psychic phone lines and services are a big no. They don't typically have qualified mediums and psychics working for them and their motivation is primarily financial, so they keep you on the line as long as possible.
- ☉ They bombard you with advertising, or ask for your credit card details before a reading.

Notes and References

Introduction: In is the Only Way Out

1. https://blogs.chapman.edu/wilkinson/2018/10/16/paranormal-america-2018/
2. https://www.forbes.com/sites/traversmark/2022/06/18/new-psychological-research-says-paranormal-experiences-are-the-norm-not-the-exception/
3. https://www.forbes.com/sites/traversmark/2022/07/01/3-paranormal-experiences-that-have-caught-the-attention-of-mental-health-researchers/?sh=10ad821b4686
4. https://noetic.org/research/extraordinary-experiences-and-performance-on-psi-tasks-during-and-after-meditation-classes-and-retreats/
5. *White Shores*, Season 6, Ep. 35: 'Accidentally on Purpose with Open Minds' with Gaia host Regina Meredith
6. Theresa Cheung, *The Afterlife is Real* (Simon & Schuster, 2011); *The Truth about Angels* (Yellow Kite, 2020)
7. Theresa Cheung, *The Element Encyclopedia of the Psychic World* (Harper Element, 2006)
8. https://www.ncbi.nlm.nih.gov/pmc/articles/PMC4086365/
9. https://www.sciencedaily.com/releases/2014/06/140623091828.htm
10. Theresa Cheung, *The Sensitive Soul* (Bookouture, 2020)
11. https://www.mpg.de/11306319/quantum-particles-in-a-synchronized-dance
12. https://www.sciencedaily.com/releases/1998/02/980227055013.htm

13. *White Shores*, Season 1, Ep. 1: 'Proof of Heaven' with Dr Eben Alexander and Karen Newell
14. *White Shores*, Season 2, Ep. 9: 'Shine On' with David Ditchfield
15. https://www.southampton.ac.uk/news/2014/10/07-worlds-largest-near-death-experiences-study.page
16. https://pubmed.ncbi.nlm.nih.gov/16484496/
17. https://hub.jhu.edu/2014/12/29/decision-making-intuition/
18. *White Shores*, Season 2, Ep. 29: 'Zenned Out' with Cassie Uhl
19. https://journals.sagepub.com/doi/abs/10.1177/2167702617728705?journalCode=cpxa
20. *White Shores*, Season 6, Ep. 27: 'Lessons and Blessings' with Melanie Tonia Evans
21. *White Shores*, Season 6, Ep. 4: 'Lottery Dreams' with Timothy Schultz
22. https://pubmed.ncbi.nlm.nih.gov/23730907/
23. https://www.scientificamerican.com/article/why-rituals-work/

Lesson One: Psyche Yourself Out

1. https://www.webmd.com/a-to-z-guides/news/20210708/you-have-a-sixth-sense-you-probably-arent-using-yet
2. https://www.amazon.com/God-Gene-Faith-Hardwired-Genes/dp/0385720319
3. J. Baptista *et al.*, 'Explicit anomalous cognition: a review of the best evidence in Ganzfeld, forced choices, remote viewing and dream studies', in *Parapsychology: A handbook for the 21st century*, eds. Etzel Cardeña, John Palmer, David Marcusson-Clavertz (McFarland and Co., 2015)
4. P. Tressoldi *et al.*, 'Extraordinary claims require extraordinary evidence: a classical and Bayesian review of evidences', *Frontiers in Psychology*, 2 (10 June, 2011)

5. B. Williams *et al.*, 'Revisiting the Ganzfeld ESP debate: a basic review and assessment', *Journal of Scientific Exploration*, 25: 4 (2011), 639ff

6. https://psychology.arizona.edu/users/gary-schwartz

7. https://med.virginia.edu/perceptual-studies/who-we-are/history-of-dops/dr-ian-stevenson/

8. *White Shores*, Season 4, Ep. 29: 'You'll Be Back' with Steve Burgess

9. *White Shores*, Season 2, Ep. 19: '*Déjà Vu*' with Robert Schwartz

10. https://med.virginia.edu/perceptual-studies/who-we-are/history-of-dops/dr-ian-stevenson/

11. https://pubmed.ncbi.nlm.nih.gov/25301715/

12. D. Bem *et al.*, 'Feeling the future: a meta-analysis of 90 experiments on the anomalous anticipation of random future events', *Journal of Personality and Social Psychology*, 100 (2011), 407–25

13. J. Utts, 'Appreciating statistics', *Journal of the American Statistical Association*, 111 (2016) 1,373–80

14. https://time.com/4721715/phenomena-annie-jacobsen/

15. https://www.webmd.com/a-to-z-guides/news/20210708/you-have-a-sixth-sense-you-probably-arent-using-yet

16. https://www.psychologicalscience.org/news/minds-business/intuition-its-more-than-a-feeling.html

17. https://pubmed.ncbi.nlm.nih.gov/16484496/

18. https://www.smh.com.au/lifestyle/life-and-relationships/sixth-sense-the-science-behind-intuition-20210304-p577wm.html

19. https://psycnet.apa.org/record/2011-01894-001

20. https://pubmed.ncbi.nlm.nih.gov/25726186/

21. https://www.frontiersin.org/articles/10.3389/fnhum.2014.00146/full

22. *White Shores*, Season 5, Ep. 13: 'Future Forward' with Dr Julia Mossbridge

23. *White Shores*, Season 4, Ep. 32: 'Just Supernormal' with Dr Dean Radin

24. https://journals.sagepub.com/doi/10.1177/0956797616629403

25. https://psycnet.apa.org/doiLanding?doi=10.1037%2Fscp0000251

26. *White Shores*, Season 4, Ep. 9: 'Your Moon Shot' with Dr Wahbeh

27. *White Shores*, Season 1, Ep. 4: 'Real Magic' with Dr Dean Radin

28. *White Shores*, Season 5, Ep. 8: 'Mind Wanderer' with Dr Arnaud Delorme

29. *White Shores*, Season 1, Ep. 8: 'Extraordinary Scientist' with Dr Loren Carpenter

30. *White Shores*, Season 5, Ep. 12: 'Good Vibrations' with Dr Garret Yount

31. http://noetic.org/science/research

32. H. Wahbeh *et al.*, 'A mixed methods phenomenology and exploratory study of channelling', *Journal of the Society for Psychical Research*, 82: 3 (2018), 129–48; H. Wahbeh *et al.*, 'Exceptional experiences reported by scientists and engineers', *Explore*, 14: 5 (2018), 329–41

33. *White Shores*, Season 1, Episodes 10 and 11: 'Science meets Spirit'

34. *White Shores*, Season 5, Ep. 18: 'From the Minds of Mediums' with Dr Julie Beischel

35. *White Shores*, Season 1, Ep. 2: 'Medium Whisperer Dr Julie Beischel'

36. https://noetic.org/research/genetics-of-psychic-ability/

37. *White Shores*, Season 1, Ep. 7: 'Professor Paranormal, Loyd Auerbach'

38. *White Shores*, Season 4, Ep. 23: 'Thunderbolt and Enlightening' with David Lorimer

39. *White Shores*, Season 2, Ep. 1: 'Lockdown Dreams' with Dr Clare Johnson

40. *White Shores*, Season 2, Ep. 31: 'Tipping Point: The New Age Movement Revealed'

41. *White Shores*, Season 6, Ep. 11: 'Holy Communication' with Revd Barry Linney

42. *White Shores*, Season 6, Ep. 1: 'Buddha at the Gas Pump' with Rick Archer
43. Theresa Cheung and Julia Mossbridge, *The Premonition Code* (Watkins, 2017), p.66 case study
44. *White Shores*, Season 3, Ep. 1: 'Let's Go Deeper' with Tim Freke
45. https://www.sciencedaily.com/releases/2017/06/170623133039.htm
46. *White Shores*, Season 3, Ep. 9: 'Clear and Present' with Martin Wells
47. https://www.health.harvard.edu/healthbeat/giving-thanks-can-make-you-happier
48. *White Shores*, Season 4, Ep. 8: 'See Your Clear Light' with Steve Taylor
49. *White Shores*, Season 3, Ep. 22: 'Is It a Wonderful Life?'

Lesson Two: Manifestations

1. *White Shores*, Season 4, Ep. 27: 'Zenned Out' with Chris Keevil
2. https://www.forbes.com/sites/alisonescalante/2021/01/28/new-science-why-our-brains-spend-50-of-the-time-mind-wandering/
3. https://www.theguardian.com/science/neurophilosophy/2012/dec/28/attention-blinking
4. https://www.ncbi.nlm.nih.gov/pmc/articles/PMC4513203/
5. https://tmhome.com/benefits/study-meditation-boosts-graduation-rates/
6. https://www.forbes.com/sites/alicegwalton/2015/02/09/7-ways-meditation-can-actually-change-the-brain/?sh=383986271465
7. https://www.health.harvard.edu/mind-and-mood/relaxation-techniques-breath-control-helps-quell-errant-stress-response
8. https://www.amp.theguardian.com/education/2010/may/03/repetitive-physics-om-improbable-research

9. https://www.researchgate.net/publication/222305048_The_Restorative_Benefits_of_Nature_Toward_an_Integrative_Framework

10. *White Shores*, Season 1, Ep. 13: 'Awakening' with Steve Taylor

11. *White Shores*, Season 2, Ep. 13: 'Living with the Land' with Dr Daniel Foor

12. *White Shores*, Season 5, Ep. 14: 'O Best Beloved' with Laura Miller

13. *White Shores*, Season 2, Ep. 6: 'Animal Whisperer Tina Read'

14. *White Shores*, Season 3, Ep. 14: 'A Man, a Dog' with David Berner

15. *White Shores*, Season 5, Ep. 24: 'A Life-Changing Resolution'

16. https://www.liebertpub.com/doi/abs/10.1089/acm.2011.0321

17. *White Shores*, Season 6, Ep. 22: 'Forget You Not' with Professor Stephen Post

18. *White Shores*, Season 6, Ep. 3: An unscheduled episode

19. H. Bosch *et al.*, 'Examining psychokinesis: the interaction of human intention with random number generators – a meta-analysis', *Psychological Bulletin*, 132: 4 (July 2006), 497ff

20. https://noosphere.princeton.edu/

21. R. Nelson *et al.*, 'Correlations of continuous random data with major world events', *Foundations of Physics Letters*, 15: 6 (December 2002), 337ff

22. *White Shores*, Season 6, Ep. 26: 'Someday is Today' with Matthew Dicks

23. *White Shores*, Season 5, Ep. 8: 'Mind Wanderer' with Dr Arnaud Delorme

24. https://psych.ubc.ca/news/wandering-but-not-lost-new-ubc-meta-analysis-unveils-the-complex-neural-correlates-of-mind-wandering/

25. https://www.forbes.com/sites/bryanrobinson/2020/09/02/why-neuroscientists-say-boredom-is-good-for-your-brains-health/?sh=693da3fb1842

26. https://www.forbes.com/sites/jennagoudreau/2012/01/30/quiet-revolution-of-the-50-percent-introverts-susan-cain/?sh=7440d7c493fb
27. Theresa Cheung, *The Moon Fix* (Quarto, 2020)
28. *White Shores*, Season 4, Ep. 10: 'Speak your Truth' with Geoff Thompson
29. *White Shores*, Season 3, Ep. 5: 'Watch your Back' with Geoff Thompson
30. *White Shores*, Season 3, Ep. 4: 'Abandoned, Pregnant' with Kandy Delor
31. *White Shores*, Season 5, Ep. 16: 'Red Dress' with Bridget Finklaire
32. *White Shores*, Season 4, Ep. 14: 'Your Only Hope' with Dr Mossbridge and Dr Sapiro

Lesson Three: Touch your Heart

1. *White Shores*, Season 3, Ep. 18: 'Something Old, New' with Peta Morton
2. *White Shores*, Season 4, Ep. 31: 'Incredible True Stories'
3. *White Shores*, Season 4, Ep. 25: 'Blue Angel Believer' with Dr Stephen Post
4. *White Shores*, Season 1, Ep. 6: 'The Scientist Who Sees the Future, Dr Julia Mossbridge'
5. https://www.researchgate.net/publication/232739694_Predictive_Physiological_Anticipation_Preceding_Seemingly_Unpredictable_Stimuli_A_Meta-Analysis
6. https://liu.se/en/article/gut-feeling-the-key-to-success
7. https://www.europeanceo.com/finance/gut-feeling-may-be-key-to-success-for-financial-traders/
8. https://www.scientificamerican.com/article/gut-second-brain/

9. https://www.psychologytoday.com/gb/blog/in-the-face-adversity/201207/thoughts-neurotransmitters-body-mind-connection

10. *White Shores*, Season 2, Ep. 12: 'Highly Sensitive Souls' with Mel Collins

11. https://www.heartmath.org/

12. *White Shores*, Season 4, Ep. 22: 'Reborn Free' with Ginny Jablonski

13. *White Shores*, Season 2, Ep. 22: 'Hidden Treasure' with Mary Ann Bohrer

14. https://pubmed.ncbi.nlm.nih.gov/16979104/

15. *White Shores*, Season 4, Ep. 18: 'Expand your Bandwidth' with Charlie Castex

16. *White Shores*, Season 5, Ep. 20: 'Extraordinary Awakenings' with Steve Taylor

17. https://www.researchgate.net/publication/265165687_Measuring_Intuition_Unconscious_Emotional_Information_Boost_Decision-Making_Accuracy_and_Confidence

18. *White Shores*, Season 3, Ep. 19: 'Feeling Too Much' with Mike Jawer

19. *White Shores*, Season 6, Ep. 8: 'Through Thick and Thin' with Mike Jawer

20. *White Shores*, Season 4, Ep. 13: 'Do It your Way' with Tim Freke

21. *White Shores*, Season 6, Ep. 18: 'Reach for your Stars' with Paul Cattermole

Lesson Four: What Dreams May Come

1. *White Shores*, Season 1, Ep. 14: 'Do You Believe in Angels?'

2. *White Shores*, Season 6, Ep. 2: 'Faculty of Divinity' with Sophie Bashford

3. *White Shores*, Season 3, Ep. 20: 'Catching Unicorns'

4. https://www.ncbi.nlm.nih.gov/pmc/articles/PMC5351796/

5. https://aphantasia.com/

6. https://pubmed.ncbi.nlm.nih.gov/10210616/

7. *White Shores*, Season 4, Ep. 28: 'A Joy Forever' with Miriam Subirana

8. *White Shores*, Season 2, Ep. 27: 'Art Becomes You' with Alena Hennessy

9. https://www.discovermagazine.com/mind/how-reading-fiction-increases-empathy-and-encourages-understanding

10. *White Shores*, Season 2, Ep. 4: 'Are You One With the Force?' with Daniel M. Jones

11. *White Shores*, Season 6, Ep. 25: 'An Endless Dream Talk' with Theresa Cheung

12. https://psycnet.apa.org/record/2019-24877-001

13. *White Shores*, Season 6, Ep. 13: 'Diving Deep into your Dreams' with Dr Clare Johnson

14. *White Shores*, Season 6, Ep. 31: 'World Dream Day' with Theresa Cheung

15. *White Shores*, Season 3, Ep. 17: 'Dream Catcher' with Dr Serge King

16. *White Shores*, Season 6, Ep. 25: 'An Endless Dream Talk' with Theresa Cheung

17. https://www.frontiersin.org/articles/10.3389/fpsyg.2013.00979/full

18. https://www.ncbi.nlm.nih.gov/pmc/articles/PMC5351796/

19. *White Shores*, Season 6, Ep. 10: 'Pure Nonsense' with Dr Julia Mossbridge and Brooks Palmer

20. *White Shores*, Season 6, Ep. 12: 'Meet Dr Sleep' with Bawa and Dinesch

21. https://www.ncbi.nlm.nih.gov/pmc/articles/PMC5768288/

22. *White Shores*, Season 6, Ep. 7: 'Your Presence, Dear' with Gary Lachman

23. *White Shores*, Season 6, Ep. 15: 'Psychic Dreams' with Loyd Auerbach

24. *White Shores*, Season 6, Ep. 9: 'True Dream Circle' with Charlie Morley

25. *White Shores*, Season 4, Ep. 12: 'Behind your Eyes' with Dr Clare Johnson

26. https://stanleykrippner.weebly.com/

27. *White Shores*, Season 6, Ep. 20: 'Your Time Loops' with Eric Wargo, PhD

28. Eric Wargo, *Time Loops* (Anomalist, 2018)

29. https://www.damer.com/

30. *White Shores*, Season 6, Ep. 23: 'Lost in Time' with Dr Julia Mossbridge

31. https://pubmed.ncbi.nlm.nih.gov/27023923/

32. *White Shores*, Season 6, Ep. 19: 'Messages from the Deep' with Dr Lauri Loewenberg

33. https://pubmed.ncbi.nlm.nih.gov/26541373/

34. *White Shores*, Season 5, Ep. 19: 'Plant Teachers' with Dr Jeremy Narby

35. *White Shores*, Season 6, Ep. 17: 'Message for All Seasons' with Joey Hullin

36. *White Shores*, Season 3, Ep. 7: 'Evil Happens' with Alex Tsakiris

37. *White Shores*, Season 6, Ep. 4: 'Lottery Dreams' with Tim Schultz

38. *White Shores*, Season 6, Ep. 30: 'In Xanadu' with Dean Sluyter

39. Do check out the 2010 Christopher Nolan movie *Inception*. You won't regret it.

40. https://www.airuniversity.af.edu/LinkClick.aspx?fileticket=p4Sg_kF-Y3w%3D&portalid=10

41. Do check out the celebrity *In Your Dreamzzz* podcast hosted by journalist and newsreader Alex Morgan and featuring myself decoding celebrities' dreams.

Lesson Five: Psychic Notes

1. *White Shores*, Season 6, Ep. 6: 'Angels are Real' with harpist Peter Sterling

2. *White Shores*, Season 6, Ep. 32: 'Dream Notes'

3. https://www.wired.com/story/tech-effects-how-does-music-affect-your-brain/

4. *White Shores*, Season 5, Ep. 21: 'An Unseen Musical Gift'

5. https://www.classicfm.com/music-news/music-gives-goosebumps/

6. *White Shores*, Season 6, Ep. 32: 'Dream Notes'

7. www.sacredacoustics.com

8. *White Shores*, Season 6, Ep. 21: 'Your Sea Soul' with Pippa Best

9. https://www.frontiersin.org/articles/10.3389/fpsyg.2021.744209/full

10. If you feel you need direction, and would like to be part of a community of mental time travellers, visit and record your daily messages via the free-to-use website, www.timemachine.love

11. https://www.ncbi.nlm.nih.gov/pmc/articles/PMC1297510/

12. https://psycnet.apa.org/record/1988-25514-001

13. Rupert Sheldrake, *Dogs That Know When Their Owners Are Coming Home* (Crown, 1999)

14. https://www.edgarcayce.org/edgar-cayce/his-life/

15. https://psycnet.apa.org/record/2019-37245-001

16. *White Shores*, Season 4, Ep. 9: 'Your Moon Shot' with Dr Wahbeh

17. Bruce Lipton, *The Biology of Belief* (Hay House, 2011)

18. https://www.ncbi.nlm.nih.gov/pmc/articles/PMC8272667/

19. https://www.ncbi.nlm.nih.gov/pmc/articles/PMC6137615/

20. *White Shores*, Season 5, Ep. 5: 'Two Vital Answers: Claire Broad and Gyles Whitnall'

21. https://noetic.org/blog/phase-1-energy-healing-study-success/

22. https://pubmed.ncbi.nlm.nih.gov/22784339/

23. *White Shores*, Season 3, Ep. 13: 'Meet Dr Strange: Dr Adam Rizvi'

24. https://adamrizvi.com/

25. *White Shores*, Season 6, Ep. 28: 'Heal' with Rodrigo Bravo

26. *White Shores*, Season 6, Ep. 33: 'Reclaiming your Wellness' with Jovanka Ciares

27. https://www.scientificamerican.com/article/why-rituals-work/

28. *White Shores*, Season 2, Ep. 3: 'Dancing Deeper' with Camilla Dallerup

29. https://pubmed.ncbi.nlm.nih.gov/22197149/

30. *White Shores*, Season 3, Ep. 2: 'The Real Vicar of Dibley' with Revd Maggy Whitehouse

31. *White Shores*, Season 2, Ep. 25: 'Brave, Beautiful and Baring It All' with Rhyanna Watson; *White Shores*, Season 2, Ep. 18 with Katie Oman; *White Shores*, Season 2, Ep. 21 with Nicole Schnackenberg

32. *White Shores*, Season 4, Ep. 10: 'Speak your Truth' with Geoff Thompson

33. *White Shores*, Season 3, Ep. 10: 'It's a Miracle' with Suzanne Clores; *White Shores*, Season 6, Ep. 39: 'Meaningful Coincidences' with Bernard Beitman MD

34. *White Shores*, Season 6, Ep. 5: 'Holy Love' with Elisa Romeo and Adam Foley

35. *White Shores*, Season 4, Ep. 21: 'Never Alone' with Dr Cassandra Vieten

36. *White Shores*, Season 5, Ep. 7: 'Losing her Leg, Finding Herself' with Ella Rose Dove

37. *White Shores*, Season 5, Ep. 22: 'Heads or Tails' with Katie B. McGrath

Lesson Six: Become your Own Oracle

1. Theresa Cheung, 'How to Be your Own Psychic', ITV *This Morning*; https://www.youtube.com/watch?v=7sNZKA86LVY

2. *White Shores*, Season 4, Ep. 11: 'Holy Hell' with Chris Johnson

3. *White Shores*, Season 4, Ep. 24: 'Blissed Out' with Greg Gorey

4. *White Shores*, Season 4, Ep. 30: 'Super People, Kate Beddow and Robin Grey'

5. *White Shores*, Season 3, Ep. 12: 'To the Stars and Back' with Phillipe Sibaud

6. *White Shores*, Season 6, Ep. 14: 'Just Ask' with Marilee Adams

Lesson Seven: Become your Own Medium

1. *White Shores*, Season 3, Ep. 15: 'Diamonds are Forever' with Dr Debra Diamond

2. *White Shores*, Season 5, Ep. 10: 'Out There, Psychic Medium Tracey Dinesch'

3. *White Shores*, Season 3, Ep. 16: 'No Place like Heaven' with Carole Obley

4. *White Shores*, Season 5, Ep. 9: 'We're Not Done Yet' with Joe McQuillen

5. https://www.nbcnews.com/better/wellness/fewer-americans-believe-god-yet-they-still-believe-afterlife-n542966

6. *White Shores*, Season 6, Ep. 11: 'Holy Communication' with Revd Barry Linney

7. *White Shores*, Season 1, Ep. 1: 'Proof of Heaven' with Dr Eben Alexander and Karen Newell

8. Theresa Cheung, *The Ten Secrets of Heaven* (Simon & Schuster, 2010), interview with Anita Moorjani

9. *White Shores*, Season 2, Ep. 9: 'Shine On' with David Ditchfield

10. https://nyulangone.org/news/recalled-experiences-surrounding-death-more-hallucinations

11. https://www.frontiersin.org/articles/10.3389/fnagi.2022.813531/full?fbclid=IwAR1lSQ6P3v9NgZVgPa3aOEfzeXJ-ISTHtyLCia2m1MsLCx-_K-Ke15Cl14Q

12. https://galileocommission.org/

13. *White Shores*, Season 4, Ep. 23: 'Thunderbolt and Enlightening' with David Lorimer

14. *White Shores*, Season 2, Ep. 11: 'Is Heaven Calling?' with Dr Mark Pittstick

15. *White Shores*, Season 5, Ep. 23: 'Paranormal Captured' with Dr Callum E. Cooper

16. *White Shores*, Season 1, Ep. 9, and Season 4, Ep. 19: 'Ghosts' with Dr Callum E. Cooper

17. *White Shores*, Season 1, Ep. 7: 'Professor Paranormal' with Loyd Auerbach

18. *White Shores*, Season 2, Ep. 10: 'From Cradle to beyond the Grave' with Ali Norell

19. *White Shores*, Season 1, Ep. 12: 'What the Dying Teach Us' with Dr Penny Sartori

20. *White Shores*, Season 6, Ep. 34: 'At Death's Door' with Dr William J. Peters

21. *White Shores*, Season 3, Ep. 6: 'Oops, I Did It Again' with Joanne Di Maggio

22. *White Shores*, Season 5, Ep. 11, 'Good Grief' with Shelley F. Knight

23. *White Shores*, Season 2, Ep. 24: 'Take my Hand' with Pat Soa

24. *White Shores*, Season 6, Ep. 29: 'Different after You' with Michele Neff Hernandez

25. *White Shores*, Season 2, Ep. 17: 'A Grief Observed' with Sasha Bates

26. *White Shores*, Season 6, Ep. 16: 'Love Changes' with Dr Matthew McKay

27. *White Shores*, Season 5, Ep. 3: 'Life to Afterlife' with Helping Parents Heal

28. *White Shores*, Season 2, Ep. 30: 'True Angel Stories'

29. *White Shores*, Season 5, Ep. 2: 'Your Afterlife Guide' with Dimitri Moraitis

30. *White Shores*, Season 3, Ep. 3: 'Real Men Do Cry' with Joe McQuillen

31. *White Shores*, Season 2, Ep. 16: 'Dying to Live' with scientifically validated medium Ankhasha

32. https://www.gaia.com/article/psychomanteum-mirror-gazing?fbclid=IwAR1lSQ6P3v9NgZVgPa3aOEfzeXJ-ISTHtyLCia2m1MsLCx-_K-Ke15Cl14Q

33. https://www.researchgate.net/publication/304986517_Anomalous_Experiences_and_the_Bereavement_Process

34. *White Shores*, Season 3, Ep. 11: 'Exhibit A from the Heart of a Law Lecturer'; Louise Hamlin, *WhatsApps from Heaven* (O Books, 2022)

35. *White Shores*, Season 3, Ep. 4: 'Abandoned, Pregnant' with Kandy Dolor

36. *White Shores*, Season 4, Ep. 16: 'It's your Afterlife'; Season 3, Ep. 8: 'Out There, Right Here' with Barry Eaton

37. *White Shores*, Season 2, Ep. 7: 'Confessions of a Medium' with Stewart Keeys

38. Theresa Cheung with Claire Broad, *Answers from Heaven* (Piatkus, 2017)

39. https://pubmed.ncbi.nlm.nih.gov/29937148/

40. *White Shores*, Season 1, Ep. 10: 'When Science Meets Spirit' with Dr Vieten and Dr Delorme; Mona Sobhoni, PhD, *Proof of Spiritual Phenomena* (Park Street Press, 2022)

41. *White Shores*, Season 2, Ep. 8: 'Everyday Mystic Kim Nash'

42. *White Shores*, Season 1, Ep. 2: 'Medium Whisperer Dr Julie Beischel'

43. *White Shores*, Season 4, Ep. 15: 'Surviving Death: Dr Julie Beischel'

44. https://pubmed.ncbi.nlm.nih.gov/25666383/
45. www.thepremonitioncode.com
46. *White Shores*, Season 6, Ep. 24: 'I See Dead People' with Dr Christopher Kerr
47. https://phys.org/news/2022-07-image-nasa-james-webb-space.html

Conclusion: You Again

1. *White Shores*, Season 4, Ep. 32: 'Just Supernormal' with Dr Dean Radin
2. *White Shores*, Season 4, Ep. 26: 'The Empowered Empath' with Wendy Da Rosa
3. https://www.researchgate.net/publication/355255498_Self-Compassion_and_Empathy_as_Predictors_of_Happiness_among_Late_Adolescents
4. https://www.psychologicalscience.org/observer/the-compassionate-mind
5. *White Shores*, Season 1, Ep. 5: 'Hearts of Darkness' with Melanie Tonia Evans
6. *White Shores*, Season 6, Ep. 37: 'The Knowing' with Jeff Olsen and Dr Jeff O'Driscoll
7. *White Shores*, Season 4, Ep. 17: 'Final Fantasy' with Dr Karen Wyatt
8. *White Shores*, Season 2, Ep. 2: 'What Truly Matters' with Dr Karen Wyatt
9. *White Shores*, Season 5, Ep. 4: 'The Earth is your School' with William Wildblood
10. *White Shores*, Season 5, Ep. 17: 'The Masks You Wear' with Peter Coyote

Inner Psychic Tools A to Z

1. *White Shores*, Season 2, Ep. 23: 'Secret of the Alchemist' with Colm Holland

2. *White Shores*, Season 4, Episodes 1 to 7: 'Days of the Week' with angel experts Alexandra Wenman and Calista

3. *White Shores*, Season 3, Ep. 21: 'Loose Angels'

4. *White Shores*, Season 2, Ep. 20: 'Your Cosmic Update' with Francesca Oddie

5. *White Shores*, Season 4, Ep. 20: 'Shooting Stars' with Amy Zerner and Monte Farber

6. *White Shores*, Season 5, Ep. 6: '*I Ching* Oracles' with Jo and Tim Dowdle

7. *White Shores*, Season 5, Ep. 25: 'Adding Everything Up'

8. *White Shores*, Season 2, Ep. 14: '11:22 Talking Numbers' with Sonia Ducie

9. *White Shores*, Season 4, Ep. 29: 'You'll Be Back' with Steve Burgess; Raymond Moody, *Coming Back* (Create Space, 2017); *White Shores*, Season 2, Ep. 15 with Lorraine Flaherty; *White Shores*, Season 3, Ep. 6 with Joanne DiMaggio

10. *White Shores*, Season 1, Ep. 3: 'Is There Anybody There?' Claire Broad and Karen Dahlman

11. https://www.vice.com/en/article/z34xa5/the-long-strange-relationship-between-psychedelics-and-telepathy

12. Theresa Cheung, *Runes for Modern Life* (Laurence King, 2019)

13. *White Shores*, Season 2, Ep. 5: 'Tarot Card Royalty' with Amy Zerner and Monte Farber

Acknowledgements

Deepest gratitude to *ITV: This Morning*, in particular Daisy Price, for taking a giant leap of faith in me for the 'Be Your Own Psychic', 'Dream Decoding' and 'Manifesting' items and viewer call-ins that inspired this book.

I am also infinitely grateful to my visionary editor, Lydia Good, to my wise agent, Jane Graham Maw (www.grahammawchristie. com), and to Alyssa, Lyndsey, Mona and Melody at Conscious Living PR for their belief, joy and positivity.

Empower your Inner Psychic would not have been possible without my previous bestselling HarperCollins dreams, birthdays, psychic world, and angel titles and the many amazing readers who messaged me over the years from their hearts about their psychic experiences. I can't thank my readers enough. You are the stuff that real dreams are made of and a never-failing source of illumination.

Gratitude also to the bold scientists and experts out there tirelessly researching dreams, consciousness and the paranormal, in particular Dr Julia Mossbridge, Dr Dean Radin and Dr Helané Wahbeh and her IONS team. I'd also like to pay tribute to every illuminating expert guest who has appeared on my podcast, *White Shores*. Your words matter. A big thank-you to Matthew Cooper and Robert Cheung for producing *White Shores* with such creative flair.

Last, but by no means least, heartfelt thanks to Ray, Robert, Ruthie and my little dog Arnie, for their love and for proving to me every single day that dreams really do come true.

About the Author

Theresa Cheung is a *Sunday Times* bestselling paranormal author. She has a degree from King's College, Cambridge University, and is the author of numerous titles which have been translated into over 40 languages, including *The Dream Dictionary from A to Z* (HarperCollins), *The Dream Decoder Card Pack* (Hachette) and *The Premonition Code* (Watkins).

Theresa works closely with scientists researching consciousness and has contributed features about dreams to newspapers and magazines such as *Bustle, Vice, Cosmopolitan, Good Housekeeping, InStyle, Red, Grazia, Heat, Glamour*, and many more. A frequent guest on *ITV: This Morning*, she has also been interviewed by Roman Kemp on Capital Radio, Regina Meredith on Gaia, Russell Brand on *Under the Skin* podcast (episode 71), George Noory on *Coast to Coast AM*, Piers Morgan on GMTV and on numerous other leading media outlets, including KTLA, Good Day Chicago, Today Extra, Channel 4 and BBC Radio. She has given dream-decoding talks and webinars for leading companies and brands, such as Beauty Bay, Anthropologie, Shiseido, Dynavision, Immediate Media, The Shift Network and the Hearst Magazine group. She also hosts her own popular podcast, *White Shores*.

You can follow Theresa on Instagram @thetheresacheung and via her Facebook and Twitter author pages, and learn more about her work at www.theresacheung.com.

'No one is you.
That is your superpower.'

Anon